S0-ADZ-428

MANAGING
FOR
SUCCESS

RICHARD IVEY
SCHOOL OF BUSINESS

MANAGING
FOR
SUCCESS

The Latest in Management Thought
and Practice from Canada's
Premier Business School

MONICA FLECK,
GENERAL EDITOR

HarperBusiness
HarperCollins*PublishersLtd*

MANAGING FOR SUCCESS

Copyright © 1999 by Ivey Management Services.

All rights reserved. No part of this book may be used or reproduced
in any manner whatsoever without prior written permission
except in the case of brief quotations embodied in reviews.

For information address HarperCollins Publishers Ltd,
Suite 2900, Hazelton Lanes, 55 Avenue Road
Toronto, Canada M5R 3L2

Artwork by Boomerang Art & Design

http://www.harpercollins.com/canada

HarperCollins books may be purchased for educational, business, or sales
promotional use. For information please write:
Special Markets Department, HarperCollins Canada,
55 Avenue Road, Suite 2900, Toronto, Ontario M5R 3L2

First Edition

Canadian Cataloguing in Publication Data
Main entry under title:
Managing for success
ISBN 0-00-200023-7
1. Management   I. Fleck, Monica.   II. Richard Ivey School of Business.
HD31.M362 1999   658.4   C98-932571-7

Printed and bound in the United States
99 00 01 02 HC 5 4 3 2 1

To Ivey faculty and alumni, and the pursuit of management excellence

RICHARD IVEY SCHOOL OF BUSINESS

Dean
Lawrence G. Tapp

Associate Dean and Executive Publisher
Kenneth G. Hardy

Publisher and Editor
Monica Fleck

Editorial Assistant
Carol Wells

The Globe and Mail

Bonnie Graham, Project Manager
Phil King, Editorial

Contents

Introduction

Sharing a vision and working together to reach that vision is essentially the message of the "Managing for Success" series. In and of itself, the series has been a project that has involved many very talented people who have added their own special touch to what has become an ongoing project with much continuing potential. Initially developed to celebrate the 75th anniversary of the Richard Ivey School of Business, the series began as a monthly supplement in *The Globe and Mail*. Today, not only is the series continuing for a second run in a national Canadian newspaper, its first series run is being commemorated in this book for distribution throughout Canada, and plans are underway to take the series to an international audience. Admittedly, this kind of success was beyond the expectations of our editorial team, but it goes to show what can be accomplished when people come together and focus their talents on a particular goal.

Our contributors, without whom none of the editorial content you are about to read would be possible, have done a tremendous amount of work behind the scenes to share with you the knowledge and advice they have accumulated. Ivey faculty and alumni have faced the challenges, issues, and very real pitfalls of our new business age, and share their lessons learned in the hopes of providing managers and executives with the information they need to have, not merely to stay in business, but to achieve continued success.

The message of the series is clear: not only do managers have to keep an eye on what's ahead on the business horizon and be prepared to react accordingly, they have to ensure that any changes in direction or strategy not only have the support of senior management across the board, but of the organization as a whole. Without the full endorsement of the organizational team, it is nearly impossible to put any new initiatives into action, at least not effectively.

Whether you're a middle- or senior-level manager in marketing, technology, finance, international business, banking, consulting, retail or a high-energy entrepreneur, there is no doubt that you know your business and you've worked hard to get where you are. The content of *Managing for Success* is geared toward such an audience and offers much for the manager who already has a good understanding of the current business environment. The issues addressed in the following chapters are designed to enhance the practice of management by providing a clear assessment of what's ahead and how this affects you and your organization, as well as concise advice on how to deal with these issues.

Selecting topics for the series presented a number of challenges. It is very difficult to select only eight areas of management practice that are significantly altering the new business age. As such, we considered a broad approach for our first series, addressing a compilation of more universal themes such as technology, leadership, marketing, and entrepreneurship, while drawing on Ivey's considerable strengths. Indeed, the theme of entrepreneurship, innovation and growth provided an opportunity for the School to showcase one of its exciting new initiatives, Ivey's Institute for Entrepreneurship, Innovation and Growth, a research and teaching center developed through a partnership of Ivey, Ernst & Young and the Bank of Montreal. The institute studies issues faced by fast-growth entrepreneurial companies in Canada and offers valuable insights, tools and strategies to help them enhance their success.

And as the business landscape is becoming increasingly crowded and boundaries are becoming more blurred, we could not overlook the opportunity to address doing business on a global basis. International strategy was our introductory issue to the international section of the series, and is also a key strength of the Ivey School, as Ivey was recently named the world leader in international strategic management research by the respected *Journal of International Management*. Our two following issues, competing in Southeast Asia and competing in the Americas, are also reflective of Ivey's continued and growing international presence. Ivey's Latin America Program has been in place for the last five years and has involved collaborations with several schools in the Latin American region, including the Instituto Panamericano de Alta Dirección de Empresa and the Pontificia Universidad Catolica de Chile. The program has also involved extensive case writing and research activities that focus on the specific issues faced by companies doing business in the Central and Latin American regions. And in September 1998, Ivey officially launched the first Hong Kong Executive MBA program in the School's satellite Hong Kong location, the Cheng Yu Tung Management Institute. The School is also recognized as the single largest producer of Asian business cases in the world and is offering a number of case-teaching workshops to educators throughout the Asian region.

The overwhelming response we received from our readers to our first run of "Managing for Success" in *The Globe and Mail* prompted us to deliver a second series, published monthly from September 1998 to May 1999. In addition to revisiting some of the themes addressed in the first series, such as entrepreneurship, innovation and growth, and technology management — key issues that continue to have a profound impact on business management — the second series takes a closer look at the ever-growing international business environment, addressing what it means to be a global player and how to navigate in a borderless marketplace. Learning about doing business in key market domains such as China, the Americas, Southeast Asia, and Europe is critical to remaining viable in the next millennium. In addition, we take a look at ourselves and how Canada stacks up as a global player in the world economy. Keep your eyes open for our next publication featuring the best of the second "Managing for Success" series.

"No manager is an island," to play on a popular phrase. Whatever you learn from the following pages can always be traced back to the concept of the buy-in, the endorsement, the team effort — whatever you choose to call it, it's the support you need to make these concepts come alive. It is our hope that this book offers you practical answers to navigating in our increasingly complex business world and how to introduce these concepts to your organization. You know how important it is to understand your business environment. And applying the latest in management thought and practice presented on the following pages to your organization's daily operations is what managing for success is all about.

Monica Fleck, General Editor

I
Entrepreneurship, Innovation and Growth: Life in the Fast Lane

Rapid Growth Businesses: Riding a Gazelle

David C. Shaw

David C. Shaw is the director of the Institute for Entrepreneurship, Innovation and Growth at the Richard Ivey School of Business.

Rapidly growing businesses are fascinating — especially for market watchers. These companies ride the boom of a new discovery, and the bets are on to see how far the organization and the entrepreneur at the helm can go, and how fast the market will accept the company's product or service. Some firms experience unprecedented growth rates. A survey of 906 CEOs of firms that were regional winners of Ernst & Young's U.S. program averaged 28 percent growth. This statistic is amazing when compared with the Fortune 500 companies average growth rate of 15 percent.

In 1988, the Canadian magazine for entrepreneurs, *Profit*, began publishing annually a list of the fastest-growing companies in Canada that have proven to be important contributors to the economy.

These organizations, in deciding to invest in products, services or technology, create additional economic value in several ways:

- The stakeholders — including the original investors, employees who participate in profit-sharing or stock option plans, the debt holders and the suppliers — share in increased profits. In 1994, Hummingbird Communications was included for the first time on *Profit's* list, ranking seventh. Specializing in PC-to-mainframe communications services, the company's sales had risen from $587,000 in 1988 to $18.0 million in 1993. In 1995, Hummingbird placed second on the list, with sales of $33.1 million; third in 1996, with sales of $63.7 million; and third again in 1997, with sales of $102.1 million. Stock was first issued to the public in August of 1993 at $16 per share. The stock reached a height of $55 in 1996, although it has since declined.
- The increased demand for the entrepreneur's product or service creates new jobs in operations, production, delivery, sales and administration. In addition, existing jobs become more stable. For example, Hummingbird grew from seven employees to 308 in its first seven years of operation.
- A successful venture stimulates investments in support industries, or related activities, creating more new jobs and more wealth.
- The business and its employees pay taxes, supporting the social benefits system. In 1995, Hummingbird paid $17.0 million in corporate income taxes and earned after-tax profits of $20.3 million after experiencing losses in 1988 and 1989.
- Rapidly growing businesses are likely to be on the leading edge of innovation, providing the economy with the means to keep up with global competition and global technological competitiveness.
- If the workforce is underemployed and if the labor pool can adapt to the skill demands of the growing business, then the economy can be boosted. Globally, for example, there is a huge shortage of skilled computer software and information technology personnel, a result of the boom in the information technology industry. A country facing underemployment could take advantage of this boom.

Often, the success of a few businesses stimulates a culture of entrepreneurial activity, resulting in the launch of more business ventures. With the associated creation of jobs, the cumulative effect of this growth can be significant. In the Ottawa-Carleton region, more than 700 companies are registered in the high-tech directory, a clear example of a community creating a culture of entrepreneurial activity.

The term coined by David Birch, the president of Cognetica Inc., to define rapidly growing businesses is "gazelles." He describes a gazelle as "a firm that is growing at 20 percent a year or better for at least five years." What this translates into is a company whose sales, by its fifth year, are two and a half times those of its base year, and that is expected to attain a 20 percent growth rate in the upcoming year. Firms that achieve 100 percent annual growth are referred to as "super gazelles."

Incredibly, when the 100 companies on *Profit*'s list were analyzed, all of the companies were gazelles — they had all achieved at least the targeted 20 percent growth rate. In 1996 data, the highest-ranked company, Oasis Technology Ltd., grew at an average annual rate of approximately 150 percent for the five years 1992 to 1996 over the 1991 base year. The company ranked 25th grew at 81 percent. Even more amazingly, the three lists from 1994 to 1996 present the greatest growth accomplishments across the whole period. Growth in sales leads to direct expectations of growth in value added and growth in jobs.

Although of the 100 companies listed in *Profit* each year, few achieved super gazelle status (as few as three in 1990 to as many as 15 in 1994), the five-year sales growth rate of these super gazelles is astonishing, averaging 5,390 percent in the nine five-year periods surveyed.

These companies were analyzed to determine if they could retain their super gazelle status in the sixth year — in other words, were the sales in the sixth year twice as large as in the fifth year? Only five Canadian super gazelles came close: FirstService Corp., Philip Environmental Inc., Alex Informatics Inc., Columbia Sportswear Canada Ltd. and Hummingbird. And these were companies that made the super gazelle list two or more years in a row based on the average sales growth rate being greater than 100 percent over the five-year period. However, only FirstService Corp. doubled sales in the sixth year after being included in the super gazelle group in the fifth year. The rest achieved an average of 100 percent over the six-year period, but failed the year-over-year test.

Interestingly, the job growth rate does not keep pace with the growth in sales, averaging 1,850 percent. While a respectable increase, this is just slightly more than a third of the sales rate. However, the job growth rate appears to be increasing — a welcome sign for the economy. In the three periods from 1994 to 1996, the job growth rate rose to about half the sales growth rate.

Where Has the Growth Occurred?

In 1996, computer-related companies began to dominate *Profit's* list of rapidly growing businesses. Other service businesses, such as call centers, also began having more of a presence on the list as of that year. Relatively few of these types of companies existed on the list in 1989. Manufacturing is now gone, but wholesale and retail, the largest segment in 1989, is still important.

The shift to more high-tech companies over the years implies products and services with shorter product life cycles. This has led to a greater need for ongoing research and development than was required by earlier gazelles.

The other startling statistic is the extent of exports for these rapidly growing Canadian businesses. In one year, nine of the top 25 businesses generated more than 80 percent of their total revenues through exports (including Hummingbird); only one exported that much seven years earlier.

Rapidly growing businesses are a significant engine of growth for the economy. Jobs, wealth creation, taxes and social benefits are linked to their success stories. Our fascination with them is well justified.

Super Gazelles

Average Sales Growth Greater Than 100 Percent a Year Over Five Years

	1987	1988	1989	1990	1991	1992	1993	1994	1995	1996
Number of Super Gazelles on List	9	4	N/A	3	9	9	6	15	11	7
Number of Jobs in These Companies										
Ending	461	422	N/A	67	1258	1206	689	12976	10891	1054
Beginning	24	29	N/A	9	68	147	40	487	536	41

Destruction and Renewal: Ethical Anarchy in Mature Organizations

David K. Hurst

David K. Hurst, writer, speaker and consultant, is currently a research fellow at the Richard Ivey School of Business. He is the author of Crisis & Renewal: Meeting the Challenge of Organizational Change, *HBS Press, 1995, from which this* Ivey Business Quarterly *article was originally adapted.*

Forest managers have learned that a mature forest must be allowed to burn if it is to be renewed. Business managers have to learn that mature organizations are the same. They need to destroy themselves — creatively — if they want to continue to succeed and survive. Destruction and renewal are imperative.

Almost every summer, large fires break out in forests across North America. News reports usually treat them as unexpected, catastrophic events. They focus on the heroic efforts of firefighters to save the forests and on the massive destruction and loss. Unusually dry conditions, high winds and lightning are usually cited as the causes of these infernos. Little attention is paid to the systemic causes, especially the attempts of governments and the timber industry to minimize the role of fire in the ecology of forests. Such practices often have perverse consequences. Until the 1970s, for example, the United States National Park Service pursued a policy of extinguishing all park fires. Its objectives were to stabilize the parks' complex ecosystems, conserving the flora and fauna for the enjoyment of park visitors.

At first the policy worked well. Small fires were easy to control. But gradually they became larger and more difficult to handle. Mature trees began to dominate the forests. Fallen leaves and branches created vast amounts of fuel. Fires could grow out of control rapidly and become catastrophic. The forest managers had actually reduced the flexibility, variety and resilience in these systems, making them dangerously unstable. Preserving the forest's complex system cannot be done by "stopping the clock." The only way such systems can survive is through constant renewal. Mature forests must burn to be renewed.

Organizations are like ecosystems; crisis is an essential part of their renewal process, as complex systems — forests and mature human organizations — have constraints. When human organizations are young, these constraints are introduced for the best of reasons — to preserve a tested method for success. But over time, as conditions change, they become a hindrance; strengths eventually become weaknesses. When such conditions arise, managers are so constrained by the system's success that they can no longer innovate within it. Their only way out of this impasse is to destroy the system — creatively — in an act of what I call "ethical anarchy." Unless they do so, they risk being overtaken by far larger "natural" disasters.

During the last 50 years, management teachings have been much more concerned with rationality in management and stability in organizations. Indeed, far from "burning" their organizations, managers have usually been preoccupied with making them "fireproof." To this day, crises and surprises are usually seen as the products of poor management.

From Life Cycle to Ecocycle

An ecosystem, such as a forest, is a dynamically stable entity. While its elements live and die, the forest survives through a continual cycle of creation, growth, destruction and renewal. It can be thought of as an ecocycle, in contrast with the more familiar life cycle that applies to individual organisms. A life cycle is generally depicted as an S-shaped curve, but the ecocycle consists of two such curves arranged to form an infinite loop. The front loop is the familiar, conventional life cycle. It tracks the system from birth through maturation to decline and crisis. The back loop is the less familiar, renewal cycle of "death" and "reconception." It begins in the confused aftermath of a crisis that shatters the constraints that bind the system and fragments the large hierarchical structures that monopolize resources. It ends with the creation of the contexts in which new organisms can flourish, setting the stage for another cycle of birth and growth.

In the ecocycle, change is continuous. Sometimes it is smooth and almost linear; at other times it is rapid and nonlinear. It is clear that renewal requires destruction. The only way to open up space in the forest is to creatively destroy the large-scale structures that monopolize its resources.

There are several parallels between the development paths of natural and human ecosystems. In both types of systems new growth emerges on the edges and in the open patches, where there is equal access to resources and little competition. In such places, a wide variety of organisms — entrepreneurs in human ecosystems — can coexist. Over time, competition breaks out in the patches as they become crowded, the more efficient species predominate while others disappear, and the overall variety of organisms in the patch falls — a process taking place in the personal computer industry at present. Eventually, growth slows as the patch becomes mature and the organisms are constrained as more and more resources are bound up inside the system and not generally available. Events are now often determined by external forces. When things are going well, managers in such organizations are usually reluctant to admit that this is the case, but when things are going badly we often read of the "circumstance beyond our control" that is held to be responsible for the problems.

There is, however, one major difference between natural and human ecosystems: Only humans can be rational, making clear choices before they act. This capacity for rational action has to be taken into account as we explore the human organization's version of the ecocycle.

The Organizational Ecocycle

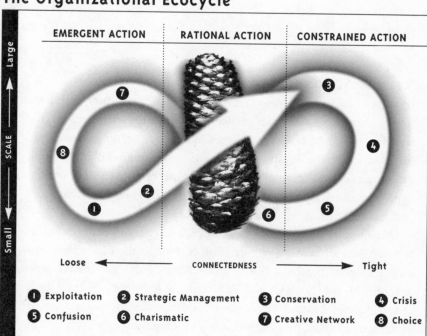

	EMERGENT ACTION	RATIONAL ACTION	CONSTRAINED ACTION

SCALE — Large ↑ — Small ↓

Loose ← CONNECTEDNESS → Tight

1 Exploitation   2 Strategic Management   3 Conservation   4 Crisis
5 Confusion   6 Charismatic   7 Creative Network   8 Choice

Traversing the Ecocycle

Phase 1: Exploitation

During the exploitation phase of the ecocycle, any available space is rapidly colonized. A forest clearing will be colonized initially by a variety of plants and other life — the "pioneers" or opportunists who take quick advantage of the open space. Similarly, in human organizations, entrepreneurs are usually opportunists. They rarely have a clear idea of what they should sell, let alone what business they are in. For example, when Bill Hewlett and Dave Packard founded their company in the late 1930s, they had no idea what products the company should make. They played around with technical challenges ranging from the control of telescope motors to a foul-line roll indicator for a local bowling alley. It took about a year for their first practical product to emerge from the laboratory at Stanford University. That product, an audio oscillator, supplied the logic that created the context for the ecocycle's next phase.

Phase 2: Strategic Management

In young organizations, managers eventually learn cause-and-effect relationships from their experiences. As with Hewlett-Packard, this learning is often a result of a series of trial-and-error experiments made when the organization was emerging. Of course, many organizations can and do imitate the apparently successful recipes of others, bypassing the trial-and-error process. Indeed, much activity and change in organizations is driven by imitation.

During this phase, what was once a successful experiment is reduced to a repeatable formula. This formula is then extended into multiple open "patches." Nike's growth during the 1970s is a classic example. Having established the company in high-performance track and field shoes, Nike managers developed products for a succession of other sports. Their progression was a combination of planning and opportunism in an unexploited field using a formula that became steadily more rational. Because the environment was unstructured, the results were almost immediately apparent. Profitable activities were extended; unprofitable ones were stopped. Here, strategies often emerge as a retrospective rationalization of what worked.

The period when the organization changes from a growth strategy to one emphasizing efficiency is critical. A new, open patch in a market favors organizations that can grow fast, but as the market matures, the fast growers risk being ousted by more efficient competitors if they cannot manage in an increasingly competitive field. From a product and technological perspective, the transition is marked by the emergence of a "dominant design" that embodies all the features that customers now regard as basic requirements. As such, its emergence often signals the end of radical product innovation in an industry or organization and a move toward improvement in the production process.

Phase 3: Conservation

Once efficiency drives the strategy and the organization becomes successful, managers will tend to restrict activities to those proven to work. Successful strategies will be elaborated upon and expanded. Often, this is accompanied by an increase in the scale of operations. The organization will specialize and emphasize efficiency, making it more successful than it might otherwise have been.

Immediately after the Second World War, the North American economy favored growth strategies in many industries. From the late 1940s to the early 1960s, there was a pent-up demand for consumer goods and a need to rebuild war-shattered Europe and Japan. By the late 1960s and early 1970s, growth began to slow. Major markets began to saturate as demand for steel, autos and housing peaked and then started to fall. By the 1980s, most of the Fortune 1000 companies were conservative structures pursuing strategies that emphasized efficiency in their domestic markets. In the process of institutionalizing their successes and pursuing efficiency, however, conservative organizations sacrifice resilience and flexibility and become more vulnerable to catastrophe.

Phase 4: Crisis — Creative Destruction

The description of the effects of a forest fire resonates with the carnage these days among what were once thought to be large, invulnerable organizations. The forest fire reduces the forest to a smoking ruin, but it creates the preconditions necessary for new elements to enter the situation, for new connections to be made, for new processes to operate and for new systems to emerge. Crisis seems to play the same role in human organizations.

Wang Laboratories' performance peaked in 1989 with more than $3 billion in revenues and a ranking of 146th in the Fortune 500. Wang had been a dominant player in dedicated word processors and their VS range of minicomputers. Three years later it filed for bankruptcy, with its common shareholders' equity all but wiped out. Wang's hierarchical structure, under which the activities of 31,500 people had once been coordinated worldwide, was destroyed as the business dwindled and divisions were closed or sold. Capital of all kinds, from asset values to employee morale to the goodwill of customers and suppliers, evaporated. Customers turned to other suppliers. Wang employees left to join other companies, form their own ventures or retire. In these new roles, many of them made a significant contribution to society. Like the nutrients and seeds that were once bound up in a large tree, with its destruction and fall they are returned to the soil to benefit the forest as a whole.

Wang's story is a familiar one in the business world. A once-successful enterprise experiences a series of setbacks, and change is precipitated by a crisis. A hectic period of "rationalization" follows, during which many parts of the business are shrunk, sold or closed. Eventually, a smaller version of the enterprise emerges, often focused on the core businesses that led to the enterprise's original success.

Such turnarounds are often necessary in organizations that have become inefficient, usually during extended periods of prosperity. But the top-down, directive management style that accompanies such activities often ensures that the business is reduced rather than renewed. There is destruction, but it may not be creative. To revert to the forest analogy, the forest has been logged, but may not have been replanted — new organisms may not have been allowed to enter the ecospace. Whereas the conventional organizational life cycle is the story of technical system's evolution, the renewal cycle is about the evolution of social systems. It is this emphasis on people and their interactions in the aftermath of crisis that allows one to explore the roots of innovation and the organizational contexts that nurture it.

Phases 5 and 6: Confusion and Leadership

Renewal begins in the confused aftermath of crisis, which shatters the previous forms of hierarchical control. Out of the confusion must emerge one or more leaders — individuals who act in ways that express their values and their beliefs about how people ought to relate to each other. Their actions are rational, not in a means-to-an-end, instrumental sense, but in the sense that their behavior consistently expresses a coherent belief system. In its most extreme manifestations we call such leadership "charismatic."

One of the best documented examples of such leadership as part of a planned effort to renew a major organization is that of Jack Welch's efforts to transform General Electric. GE was not in any apparent trouble at the time, so Welch created a pre-emptive crisis. Shortly after becoming CEO in 1981, he announced that each GE business had to be either first or second in its market or it would risk disposal. This statement was widely criticized as strategically naive. But it was not a rational statement of strategy; it was an emotional "call to arms," directed at getting the complete attention of the senior management group. Welch reinforced this message with action, delayering the management hierarchy, reducing corporate staff and slashing 100,000 employees to focus on what he believed to be the core elements of the business.

It is the confused aftermath of this "shakeup," this creative destruction, that sets the stage for the values-based behavior called charismatic leadership. Now, managers have to live the values they espouse. Their action is rational, not because it is a means to an end, but because it is intrinsically valuable. Managers in this phase are models of the behavior they expect from others. They create the crisis, but then they have to join their followers in living out the consequences. It is anarchy, but it is ethical anarchy.

This values-based, rational action is essential to attracting creative people and creating contexts that nurture innovation and entrepreneurship. Charismatic leaders attract followers who themselves can learn to lead. This allows a network of relationships to form, held together by shared values and an emerging vision of common purposes. With the emphasis on learning and the options it generates, the ability to choose is now restored to the renewed organization.

Phases 7 and 8: The Creative Network and Choice

The logic of the renewal cycle suggests that, for GE to be successful, groups of individuals must gel around various opportunities and projects, and must start to take entrepreneurial action. The individuals will interact with each other on the "boundary-less" networks developed in the contexts created by Jack Welch and his senior managers. In keeping with the emergent quality of activities in these phases of the

ecocycle, the formation of small work groups and the projects themselves will seem spontaneous and lucky, rather than planned.

The cycle should progress in much the same way as it did at Blue
Ribbon Sports (BRS) when Phil Knight and Bill Bowerman went
through the creative process for the first time on their way to invent-
ing Nike. Then, the organization had no permanent employees. A
loosely connected network of athletes and suppliers was forming,
anchored and sustained by the visions and passions of Knight and
Bowerman. They were the nucleus of a new social system that would
invent a new technical system.

To an outside observer at that time, the organization would have
been invisible or, at the very least, diaphanous. One would have
looked right through it and seen only a social network. Yet this was
when BRS was the most acutely sensitive to its environment, and
when small, insignificant events had significant consequences. That
is why, in retrospect, the "founding" of the business often appears to
consist of a series of unpredictable events and chance encounters
with helpful people.

With Nike, over time, the loosely connected network began to
pulse in a pattern. If one had attended the track meetings where the
athletes gathered to compete (and talk about their equipment), one
might have observed how, after a brief bonding period, the patterns
in the loosely connected network began to change. Using new distribution channels and some contacts they had made, Knight and
Bowerman began to sell their shoes to a wider market. A more regular pattern of interactions began to emerge as the contacts and events
became linked into coherent flows and better-articulated routines.
Soon a small, simple, but permanent structure formed and moved
into the next phase of the ecocycle. At about this time, although
insignificant in size, it became clearly visible to outside observers and
was ready to be named. Nike was on its way.

Crisis and Creation

Yet many managers are disturbed by the notion that organizational
renewal requires crisis. In human organizations, destruction is likely
to seem creative only to those who are either at one level above the
system being destroyed or outside the situation altogether. Observers

can agree that trees must burn to renew the forest and that organizations must fail if an industry is to remain competitive. It is the people inside the system who are the subjects of change, and the resulting feelings of fear and uncertainty contrast unfavorably with the feelings of control and even omnipotence that characterized the previous phase of the organizational ecocycle. It is no wonder that managers usually talk about making their businesses "fireproof."

Indeed, Intel is a company that has continually renewed itself in "open patches" created by technological change. In the 1980s crisis played a major role in forcing them to abandon their memory chip business, which had been the foundation of their success, and facilitating a move to the then-new microprocessor business. As memory chips had become commodities, Intel found itself unable to differentiate its memory offerings and began to lose money and market share to the Japanese. The wrenching decision to abandon the technology drivers, thought to be at the root of their success, was catalyzed by crisis. Similarly, in the mid-1990s the "Pentium Flaw" crisis, a seemingly minor error in Intel's new microprocessor chip, promoted a radical revision of Intel's (and the industry's) quality standards for both hardware and software products.

The approach used by 3M yields a different perspective. This company appears to have institutionalized the systematic "burning" of its mature businesses using internal methods. They insist that all divisions generate at least 30 percent of their sales from products introduced within the past four years. At the same time, the organization's culture clearly encourages extracurricular activities — for example, they allow employees to spend up to 15 percent of their working time on personal projects. The well-known story of the evolution of the Post-it™ note and its initial rejection by senior management suggests even more subtle cultural aspects of 3M that facilitate the mobilization of their people's talents. Far from making their businesses fire-resistant, 3M's reliance on crisis seems to make them fire-dependent. Exposure of the businesses to the environment allows them to be renewed.

But what is the "it" that survives during renewal and allows us to say that an organization has been renewed? "It" is not the people or their possessions, the customers or the suppliers. "It" is not the physical or legal structures, products or technologies. All these can and will change.

"It" can only be non-physical "things" — shared beliefs, stories, memories, visions and values. Only they have the capacity to create meaning and inspire people — to regenerate and renew an organization.

This is true of people who once worked for any organization to which they felt an emotional attachment. When everything else is gone, they will still remember the visions, values and social contexts that once inspired the commitment of thousands to work together. Wherever they are, these contexts may be recreated and knowledge of them passed on to the next generation. Thus "the company" remains as patterns of interaction in an immense network, vast beyond our comprehension. But through this network, the patterns have the potential to be reincarnated in new, formal organizations at any time.

Perhaps, in the long run, this is the only sense in which any human organization survives.

Adapted and reprinted with permission from Harvard Business School Press. From Crisis and Renewal: Meeting the Challenges of Organizational Change *by David K. Hurst. Boston, MA, 1995. Copyright © 1995 by David K. Hurst, all rights reserved.*

Improvise to Innovate

Mary Crossan

Mary Crossan is a professor of strategic management at the Richard Ivey School of Business and has done extensive work on improvisation through Ivey's partnership with The Second City.

Improvisation is nothing new in the world of comedy entertainment. For years, The Second City Improvisational Company of Toronto and Chicago has entertained thousands, bringing the likes of such comedians as John Candy and Gilda Radner to our television and movie screens. But improvisation is not a skill many of us have considered using at the office. After all, what does being spontaneously funny have to do with business? The similarities and applications may be greater than you think. Not only does improvisation provide a way to understand what it takes to be spontaneous and innovative, but applying these skills in the workplace allows an organization to be more effective and responsive. Improvisation may be the very skill that helps entrepreneurial managers maintain their competitive edge.

Many parallels exist between the theatrical stage and the boardroom: traditional theater uses a script to guide the performance; sets, costumes and props enhance the story-line; actors are selected for their likeness to particular characters; and, as leader, a director ensures that all elements support one another. Except for their applause, the audience has no input into the performance. In business, the strategy operates like a script, guiding the organization's actions under the CEO's direction. Individuals are hired to fill particular roles, and numerous assets support the business activity. Unfortunately, many businesses allow customers about as much input as the audience of a play. And like many plays, such businesses usually have a limited run.

But improvisational theater is the counterpoint to traditional theater. Improvisation uses no sets, costumes, props or scripts, and the actors play a variety of roles. The audience participates by providing input to the story. Rather than directing the performance in the traditional sense, the director helps the actors reflect on the performance.

Second City and the Ivey Business School teamed up to investigate what it takes to improvise and how it differs from more traditional approaches of learning and strategic renewal. We discovered that the exercises used by actors to develop their improvisational skills can be adopted by business as a means to experience and enhance the individual's and the organization's ability to be innovative and responsive.

Why Improvisation?

The only sustainable competitive advantage for companies, suggests Arie DeGeus, a former senior planner at Royal Dutch Shell, is their ability to learn faster than their competitors (DeGeus, A. 1988 "Planning as Learning," *Harvard Business Review*, March/April, 70–74). But what tools or technologies do we need to take us beyond being just good managers to becoming innovative managers? Improvisation may be one way of thinking about and developing the new skills needed to succeed in today's fast-moving and highly competitive environment.

While planning has its place, many companies rely too much on the planning process, which involves long-time horizons before action occurs, and requires much analysis in its development. Managers need to learn how to respond faster and offer more innovative solutions. With speed comes a need to operate more spontaneously.

"Planning has had its day," according to Henry Mintzberg, who concluded from his study of managerial work two decades ago that 90 percent of what managers do is spontaneous in nature. However, this does not mean that their actions are creative; much of what managers do is more like transacting. But if tomorrow is going to be better than today, then today's actions need to be more intuitive, creative and innovative. People need to learn to apply creativity and intuition to their daily actions. Improvisation, with its key aspects of spontaneity and intuition, offers the needed solution.

Six Areas to Develop

Six key areas, if developed, can contribute to a manager's ability to improvise: interpreting the environment, crafting strategy, properly nurturing individual skills, cultivating leadership, fostering teamwork and assessing organizational culture.

1. Interpreting the Environment

The book *Border Crossings* describes an Ivey Business School study about successful Canadian companies that failed in their attempts to enter the U.S. market. A key challenge facing these companies was interpreting the competitive environment. They failed to see what, in hindsight, were clear signals. Karl Weick, a noted management researcher, suggested that this happens because managers tend to "see what they believe" rather than "believe what they see." The challenge then is to go beyond the current way of thinking in order to see things differently. In a recent *Fortune* article, "Killer Strategies," Harvard professor Gary Hamel noted that competitors from outside an industry are often the ones who change the face of competition within the industry — precisely because conventional views do not constrain them.

When forced to respond or act quickly, people usually rely on left-brain analytical thinking because it is familiar and automatic. A premise of improvisation is that traditional mindsets can be broken by relying more on right-brain or creative thinking. By carrying out actions that seem contradictory, one can ease the natural tendency to shift into analytical mode. A variety of improvisational exercises have been designed to enable individuals to experience this shift in thinking. For example, one exercise, called "Nonsense Naming," requires individuals to walk around the room quickly and give every object a name that is something other than what it is. This may sound easy, but spontaneously calling an object something different from what you have experienced all your life is difficult. Even when they do come up with a new name, people are often locked into viewing the object within a particular category; for example, they call a table a chair. This highlights a serious problem in business: if we have such difficulty calling a table something other than a chair, how difficult is it for companies to identify new competitors, different customer needs, or different ways of getting a new product on the market? Even when individuals can break out of traditional mindsets, they often bump up against the organization, which is unable to deviate from a defined strategy.

2. Crafting Strategy

Mintzberg made an important distinction between intended, emergent and realized strategy. Intended strategy is that with which we are all familiar. The annual plan sets out how the organization will position itself within the competitive environment over the coming three to five years. It expresses the organization's goals, defines the products it will offer and the markets it will serve, and presents the basis of its competitive advantage.

In contrast, emergent strategy comes from the day-to-day activities of the organization. Today's business education cultivates skills that support the development of intended strategies. Improvisation builds on the types of skills that support the development of emergent strategies. Ultimately, the organization's strategy is a blend of both intended and emergent, but, unfortunately, many organizations do not have the capacity to let that combined strategy emerge. 3M is a notable exception; its management actively encourages the development of new products, which they hope will renew the company's strategic orientation.

The equivalent of emergent strategy in improvisation can be seen in the way actors develop storylines spontaneously. An exercise called "Make a Story" requires a group to build a story, one person at a time. The audience provides the story's title and category (a murder mystery or an adventure, for example). A conductor leads the ensemble, pointing to one person at a time who then builds the story in short increments. The challenge is to build an interesting and coherent storyline. Many people have a strong tendency to try to control the story by planning where they want to take it, rather than building on each other's ideas.

3. Fostering Teamwork

The intent and desire to let strategies or storylines emerge are important. But a high degree of teamwork is also needed, something many organizations have already recognized. Improvisation provides a slightly different perspective on teamwork. Enabling people to collectively respond in the moment requires what improvisers call "yes anding." A fundamental premise of improvisation, "yes anding" means that individuals build on, rather than block, each other's ideas. Senior management of an organization undergoing dramatic, strategic change states that, as they go through the shift, the answer to any questions posed is to be "yes" or "maybe." This approach ensures the continuity of the change, which can be a very challenging process. Although wanting to encourage forward movement by saying yes, they also want to encourage dialogue and reflection by using "maybe" to reconsider requests.

Besides "yes anding," improvisation highlights the importance of having a common goal. In an exercise called the "Imaginary Tug-of-War," two teams try to recreate a realistic representation of a tug-of-war. Undoubtedly, the urge to win overwhelms the groups. The result is almost inevitable: each group heaves back, stretching the imaginary rope in both directions.

4. Developing Individual Skills

Although good improvisation needs to foster teamwork, it also requires the development of the individual's skills. Researcher and professor Guy Claxton suggested that the desire to be consistent, competent, comfortable and confident are key barriers to learning (*Live and Learn: An Introduction to the Psychology of Growth and Change in Everyday Life*, Harper and Row Publishing, 1984). Control should be added to his list. Improvisation challenges these tendencies.

Responding creatively and intuitively in the moment by building on others' ideas requires that individuals think and act in ways with which they are uncomfortable. For most people, this is a tremendous psychological challenge. Improvisation's spontaneous nature taxes the basic skills of listening and communicating. It demands that individuals give their full concentration and attention to the moment, rather than being preoccupied by what happened or what could happen.

Improvisation also demonstrates that, to be convincing, one must be committed. Whether an audience in improvisational theater or a customer in business, it is striking how supportive people will be of a person giving everything they can to make something happen, even when problems arise.

5. Cultivating Leadership

Because in improvisation different people take the lead at different times, the ability to both lead and follow must be developed. Players must expand their set of competencies in order to take on a variety of roles. No leadership role is defined; people must make their own judgments about when to get involved, what to offer and when to redirect the scene. This is contrary to the hierarchical management style of many companies.

The improvisational exercise "Switch" shows the challenges associated with shifting leadership. Two individuals begin to play out a scene. When one observer sees an opportunity to step in, he or she calls "freeze" and replaces a player by assuming his or her physical position. The new player restarts the action, taking the scene in an entirely new direction. Individuals must be alert to the opportunities in the situation and what they can offer to move the scene forward. When a new person enters, the person remaining must be ready to support the new direction.

6. Assessing Organizational Culture

Developing each of the key areas is highly dependent upon an organizational culture that supports improvisation. The systems, structures, procedures and operating practices of organizations are more likely to impede it. How easy is it in your organization for an innovative idea to be implemented? How often do you see people throughout the organization demonstrating leadership or taking some risk in what they do? The lack of improvisation may be because reward systems discourage — or worse yet, punish — risk-taking. Or a lack of teamwork may arise from an organizational structure that has outgrown its usefulness. Shortcomings in current structures and systems manifest themselves in the organization's overall culture or feel. Is the organization cold, dull and uninspiring, or is it vibrant, exciting and challenging?

Although these elements are perhaps the hardest to change, deficiencies create an uphill battle for individuals and groups trying to foster improvisation. One frustrated CEO in the Second City/Ivey study noted the lack of initiative and risk-taking by his company's employees. Yet nothing encouraged or endorsed such behaviors except a few words by the CEO, words that could not overcome decades of practice to the contrary.

While business culture generally dictates professionalism, a culture of friendship exists in improvisation. In improvisation, people care about one another and support each other's efforts, cultivating a high degree of trust. A culture of friendship in business means that individuals think about setting up the next person for success.

However, improvisation requires taking risk, which in turn requires patience and even tolerance for error by both the customer and the organization.

Implementing Improvisation

Different areas of an organization provide different opportunities to improvise. A challenge is assessing the organizational culture, determining where and how innovation and improvisation can occur.

Implementing improvisation does not require rejecting what companies have been doing. On the contrary, companies need to sharpen their traditional skills and add to them. Improvisation builds on a strong set of basic skills. In music, to master his or her instrument, a jazz musician needs to develop and practice the same basic skills as a classical musician. But to improvise, the musician needs an added skill set.

Managers who want to implement an improvisational approach should begin by developing their own capacity to improvise and cultivating their own leadership skills to step in where required. The next step is extending these skills to the team.

Faster, better, smarter is not just more of the same. Like world-class theatrical plays or orchestras, organizations need to master basic traditional skills, but they need to do more if they are to be as innovative and responsive as the jazz musician. Improvisation provides a pathway to understand and begin acting on what it takes to innovate.

Reprinted with permission from Ivey Business Quarterly

Employee Compensation: Attracting and Retaining Key Players

Brian Golden and Nancy Roberts

Brian Golden is a professor of organizational behavior at the Richard Ivey School of Business. Nancy Roberts is a research project manager at Ivey's Institute for Entrepreneurship, Innovation and Growth.

Entrepreneurial companies, particularly those experiencing rapid growth, need innovative compensation policies. With most of their money tied up in the development of products or services, these companies are left with very little for traditional compensation plans. But given that they are competing in increasingly dynamic markets, they need people who are experienced and highly talented.

A high-tech, rapidly growing company found that their engineering graduates, after two years with the firm, were being hired away by large corporations, such as Nortel and Microsoft. Although they were happy with their employer, the combination of excellent training in the first two years after graduation with the high-tech company and robust demand for people with engineering skills, made these employees highly valuable on the outside. While the company was experiencing rapid growth and pressures on cash, and its key employees were buying homes and starting families, larger, more established corporations were aggressively looking for employees and offering large salaries. These key employees often found the certainty of large salaries today preferable to even greater pay in the future — if the entrepreneurial company succeeded.

As the example shows, rapid growth and other entrepreneurial companies face several unique problems. The talent that they need to hire costs money, which the company most likely does not have in abundance, and may not have any time soon. They are busy pumping funds into research and development, advertising and promotion, new buildings and equipment, distribution systems, customer service and data-gathering systems — the list can seem endless. As a result, a long time can pass between the time when merit pay or a bonus is earned and when the company can pay it out. Also, entrepreneurial companies often have difficulty paying for the credentials and quality of work they need from an employee. Simply put, larger companies are typically able to offer more attractive pay and benefits.

Second, once entrepreneurial companies have hired these key employees, they need ways to keep them satisfied, loyal and committed to the goals of the company — no easy task when your rate of growth is shooting through the roof. The demands on a person's time and energy can be growing as quickly as the firm. Working weekends and nights can become the norm. Managers are busy making quick decisions in their constantly changing environment, and need to know that they will be rewarded based on how much risk they face daily. Setting compensation targets that are realistic, given the economic realities of the company, and having the employees agree to these targets, can be challenging.

Stock options are often proposed as means to compensate key employees without giving up currently scarce cash. However, entrepreneurs are usually reluctant to give up ownership in their company. One private company that tried offering stock options found that its young key employees wanted cash; non-liquid, long-term stock options were not helpful for down payments on houses, student loan repayments, new family-style vehicles and other immediate-satisfaction expenditures. However, another private company refused stock options to divisional CEOs and offered profit-based bonuses instead, only to find that these senior officers sought other employment opportunities that offered participative equity.

As the first part in a research series to be conducted on key employees, the Institute for Entrepreneurship, Innovation and Growth at the Ivey Business School reviewed the compensation plans of more than 100 companies experiencing rapid growth to find out how they compensate their key employees and how successful their plans are at fulfilling their strategies. By looking at the fastest-growing companies (we selected from companies that had appeared on *Profit* magazine's list of the top 100 fastest-growing companies in Canada), we hoped to discover just what was working for them, in the hopes that their success could be applied elsewhere. We wanted to learn what they were doing that was different from normal growth companies.

A key employee was defined as someone who performs a role — strategic or operating — that is critical in sustaining the business' ongoing viability. Such an employee would not be easily replaced. For example, many respondents considered their organization's chief financial officers as key employees, who, if lost to other firms, would pose very significant problems for an entrepreneur/owner in both the loss of critical communication of key operating information to the officers, the bank and other investors, and the loss of confidence of the owner.

How Do Entrepreneurs Pay Their Key People?

Rapid growth businesses use a variety of compensation practices. Most respondents pay key employees a salary, but also use several other performance-based compensation methods to reward these employees. In fact, entrepreneurs expressed the view that salary should be about 65 to 75 percent of total compensation. Profit-sharing was the most often used method (72 percent of companies), but bonuses, commissions and stock options were also frequently used. How much profit was assigned to key employees was based on a percentage formula — between the 10 and 25 percent range, with 20 percent as the most quoted rate. Bonus amounts were normally based on the company owner's discretion.

If you are entrepreneurial, how can you compete? We agree with the human resources consultants at Ernst & Young, partners with the Bank of Montreal and Ivey in forming the institute, who emphasize that firms should align compensation strategies with overall business strategies. Since compensation plans affect corporate culture, consideration should be given to determining what culture is desired in the future before changing the existing compensation program.

John Johnston, a principal in the human resource consulting practice at Ernst & Young, advises, "Consider the needs and requirements of your truly key employees carefully. Make sure that you pay competitively [by constantly checking your market data] but also recognize that sometimes jobs are defined by these key performers. Focus on paying the person, not just the box on the organization chart."

While it is important to know the market's compensation levels for key employees, a rapidly growing business may choose other levels or a different mix of pay variables to pay its key employees. Different markets exist for different types of employees. For example, high-tech computer software engineers are currently compensated according to levels determined in the United States, but local or regional markets may govern the type of compensation offered to sales, clerical and professional employees.

Employees who are truly key to a rapidly growing business may require a compensation scheme that ensures long-term employment. Stock options or bonuses with deferred payout may give them the incentive they need to remain with the company. "It is now as important to consider how you pay key people, not just how much you pay," says Johnston.

Base Salary

The first step in developing a compensation plan aligned to a growth strategy is to determine how much cash key employees should be paid. This involves thoroughly researching competitors' pay programs as tempered by local conditions, determining the importance of the job to the firm and evaluating the special role requirements or skills of the job. Once the compensation amount is determined, how fixed pay, salary and benefits are to be mixed with variable pay, profit-sharing and other performance-based rewards can be assessed. The variable compensation component provides the incentive and motivation for the employee to achieve corporate objectives and share in both the risks and the rewards. However, a mix of too much variable compensation and too little fixed compensation may result in massive resignations during a bad year. This is especially true when some external factor other than employee effort, such as economic conditions, is to blame.

Variable compensation programs require care in their inception to ensure that they are consistent with the firm's goals. Once instituted, the communication with employees must be timely, frequent, meaningful and consistent. The rules for measurement must be clear and must be followed. Full and timely disclosure is critical to the success of the plan. "If a manufacturing company decides to pay for increased production and achieves significant increases in output, it must also consider that it needs to sell the excess production. If finished goods inventory rises it will cost the company not only the additional compensation but also the cost of keeping the inventory," Johnston says. "Careful design and thorough testing can avoid serious pitfalls."

If they have the knowledge and support of employees, rapid-growth businesses can probably postpone establishing a full-blown compensation plan while they struggle through the problems of corporate survival. However, once they achieve success, then these key employees expect to be rewarded for their efforts. Entrepreneurs/owners must introduce a compensation package that not only rewards, but satisfies and excites.

Welcome to the Innovation Age

Mary Jane Grant

Mary Jane Grant is a professor teaching creativity in business at Ivey's Institute for Entrepreneurship, Innovation and Growth.

The path to success offers no shortcuts, nor can greatness simply be re-engineered into an organization. Although managers are aware they need to find more creative solutions to their problems, many businesses still lack an innovative environment that fosters creativity. If companies are waiting for proof that innovation is profitable, they may now have it. The Innovation Age has arrived...and it pays.

What Is Innovation?

Innovation is a purposeful process driven by creativity through all stages of development and implementation. The results are clearly defined and measurable business outcomes. Teresa Amabile offers the simplest and most widely accepted definition of innovation. She states it is "the successful implementation of creative ideas within an organization" (*Harvard Business*

Review, 1996). Note that this definition requires the successful implementation of ideas. It is important to ask at every stage, "Where is this exercise leading us?" and "Toward what specific outcome are we applying this innovation process?" Successful implementation is the discipline built into innovation's core.

Innovation should be preceded by the generation and capture of creative ideas. Without creative people, there can be no innovation. For innovation efforts to be successful, one cannot afford to have a laissez-faire attitude toward creativity. Creativity must be nurtured; you cannot wait for when and if it comes along. You need to encourage a creative process that is purposeful, continuous and goal-directed. You will still have serendipitous ideas, but you need more than this if you are going to drive a productive and sustainable innovation process.

Innovation is not restricted to new product development. It is relevant throughout the organization, applying equally well to the cost side and the revenue side of the business. Innovation that creates value for the bottom line can occur anywhere in an organization and can be applied to all aspects of internal and external operations.

Any enterprise that believes it can exist without innovation is denying the basic premise on which it was founded. Every product and company originated with a creative idea, discovered through hard work, luck or even by accident. This idea was captured and developed, probably in the face of skepticism and self-doubt at times, to the point where it was successfully introduced into a new or existing marketplace. The greater the ultimate impact and success of the product, the more challenge it likely faced during its early stages of growth and development. Indeed, innovation is and always has been the driving force behind sustained business success.

Innovation Fuels Revenue Growth

Every company seeks growth. One of the most powerful determinants of growth is innovation. It is widely understood that if you have nothing new to offer the market, you will eventually be left behind by the competition. Today, more than anecdotal evidence exists on the linkage between innovation and growth than ever before.

Research in both the United States and Canada is producing results of considerable magnitude. U.S. research studies have shown that innovative companies experience growth rates that are twice as great as those for non-innovative companies. In addition, a new Statistics Canada study of 3,000 Canadian firms finds that faster-growing companies are almost twice as likely to innovate as slower-growing firms. This study also finds that the linkage between innovation and growth holds up across industry category or the firm's age. It concludes that "...regardless of the industry in which the firm operates or the maturity of the market in which the firm serves, innovators grow faster than non-innovators."

And innovation is not simply about growth, but about growth that translates into value for the bottom line. Several years ago, chemical conglomerate Du Pont, considered a pioneer in innovation, made innovation a deliberate and consciously managed function in their company. Even today, this type of approach is unusual in most companies, where innovation is still very much a random act. The results, as reported by R.H. Tait at the May 1997 conference of the American Creativity Association, show Du Pont has found:

- a 35 to 50 percent improvement in development cycle time;
- a 25 to 35 percent reduction in per-project development costs;
- that 40 to 50 percent of projects have been rationalized; and
- that a continuous stream of new products has enhanced revenues.

Another new study has found that the payoff from innovation is directly related to the magnitude of innovation. In a study of the product launches of 100 companies, researchers W. Chan Kim and Renee Mauborgne (*Harvard Business Review*, 1997) discovered that 86 percent of launches were line extensions (incremental improvements in a product), accounting for 62 percent of total revenues and 39 percent of profits. The remaining launches were considered significant innovations or breakthrough changes that generated only 30 percent of total revenues, but 61 percent of profits.

So, not only is innovation the engine of growth, but the more significant the innovation, the higher the potential rate of return.

Employees Prefer Innovative Workplaces

Innovative companies are more satisfying places to work. In a study of 288 bank employees reported in *Applied Psychology* (1993), higher degrees of innovation within a group were associated with lower levels of turnover among employees. Lower turnover and higher satisfaction result in increased productivity. Organizations that create more innovative workplaces reap the benefits of more productive workforces.

After R. J. Reynolds' research and development group implemented a culture change and a training program designed to significantly enhance innovation, they not only experienced much greater productivity in terms of new products and processes, but they also moved into the top 10 percent of U.S. manufacturing firms in a survey of positive workplace culture. In addition, the group showed a 20 percent improvement in their own measures of teamwork, respect, employee involvement, cooperation and support and, of course, innovation and risk-taking.

With such big payoffs as growth, profitability and productivity, who could resist making innovation a bigger part of their business? Almost everyone, it would appear. One study has found that, while 80 percent of U.S. executives feel that innovation is critical to their companies' survival, only 4 percent feel their companies are superior at making innovation happen.

It used to be that executives would say, "I don't want a bunch of creative thinkers around here...they'll just get distracted from the business." Today, these same executives are realizing that creativity and innovation are an integral part of continued success. The proof is in, and attitudes are changing.

II
Technology Management:
Facing the Challenges

Aligning Information Systems Strategy with Business Strategy

Sid L. Huff and Yolande E. Chan

*Sid L. Huff is a professor of
management science and information systems at the Richard
Ivey School of Business and the
holder of the Hewlett-Packard
Chair in Information Technology
Management. Yolande E. Chan
is a business professor at Queen's
University and holds a Ph.D.
from Ivey.*

Many studies have been conducted to determine
how important information systems issues are
to organizations. But from year to year, study to
study, the issue that seems to matter most to everyone
is how to align the company's IS strategy with its
business strategy. Executives seem to have an almost
visceral sense that, if one is to use information technology to maximum effectiveness, then strategic IS
alignment must supersede almost everything.

At one time, information systems professionals were often accused of not understanding — or even caring about — the businesses that employed them. But today's IS professional appears to have recognized the competitive environment in which his or her company operates, and, as a result, has become more cognizant of and focused on business. Today, applications are developed jointly, the need for corporate sponsors for significant IS projects has been recognized, and IS as well as non-IS managers move in and out of roles in the IS department. These practices indicate that firms have reached a level of awareness — the first of three levels — in achieving a state of strategic IS alignment.

What follows from level one is a need to integrate the organization's operational plans with those of IS. Most often, IS plans are formulated following the creation of the company's business plans. But some organizations — especially those in information-intensive industries that recognize how central their information resources are to their businesses — develop business and IS plans simultaneously. This approach makes possible much tighter integration of IS into the core requirements of the organization.

In a few organizations, IS opportunities drive business development. Examples range from tiny, niche-market startups to large airlines, such as AMR Corporation.

At the third level, in which strategic alignment is reached, integration is taken one major step higher. Whereas the second level is concerned with integrating operational business and IS plans and activities, the strategic alignment level concerns integrating IS with the organization's fundamental competitive strategies and core competencies.

Consider a financial services firm that plans to launch a new type of mortgage for potential homeowners. With strong integration (second level), such a firm would have developed its operational plans for the new mortgage product in close concert with specific IS plans for creating and supporting the information systems necessary to offer the product. However, if the firm has strong IS strategic alignment, it would understand that one of its core strategic thrusts was the frequent creation and introduction of innovative financial products for its customers. Consequently, the firm would have, over time, directed significant IS resources toward building the capability of effectively supporting this strategic thrust, perhaps through investment and training in rapid-application development tools, such as object-oriented programming tools.

To determine how important IS strategic alignment is and how it is achieved, we contacted 170 North American–based companies in two major industrial sectors: manufacturing and financial services. We began by creating a way to measure business strategy, IS strategy and strategic alignment. To measure business strategy, we used MIT management scholar N. Venkatraman's way of characterizing a business' strategy as a collection of seven strategic orientations: aggressiveness, analysis, defensiveness, futurity, innovativeness, proactiveness and riskiness. For each of the seven dimensions, we created a set of questions to determine the extent to which a company's information systems supported that dimension of its business strategy.

We were then able to define precisely, and actually measure, the degree of IS strategic alignment in a given organization. In a similar fashion, we developed and tested measures for effectiveness and business performance. For the latter we looked at four aspects of performance: financial performance, market growth, product-service innovation and company reputation.

We found that IS strategic alignment is not a "nice to have" feature, but rather, is critical to organizational effectiveness. The most exciting and managerially relevant finding was the relative importance of alignment to both IS effectiveness and business performance. The strongest relationships in the entire model were those between alignment and business performance, and between alignment and IS effectiveness.

Managers should therefore take the strategic alignment challenge as seriously as possible. They should direct resources toward achieving improved alignment — and should not skimp. Consider alignment implications before moving ahead to implement strategic plans.

We found that alignment was somewhat more complicated than simply calculating the difference between each of the seven pairs of measures. In essence, we discovered that the stronger the strategic profile dimension, the more important good alignment becomes. For example, say a company's strategic profile exhibits high aggressiveness and the company provides a high degree of IS support for aggressiveness. This combination would contribute proportionally much more to business performance and IS effectiveness than would low aggressiveness and corresponding low IS support for aggressiveness. It involves more than a simple match.

Managers should determine which dimensions of their organization's strategy matter most, then direct IS resources to support those dimensions first.

Our data also showed that firms should not totally ignore any of the seven strategic dimensions. Even in cases where an organization registers very low on one or more strategic dimensions, a minimal level of IS support for that dimension is better than no support. Establish a baseline of IS support for all aspects of strategy, and then move from there to add more support to those dimensions that are most important.

Traditionally, information systems have focused mainly on providing support for analysis and action, and not for planning. When we examined our data, however, we found that, in general, the organizations with the most effective IS functions were those that directed their IS resources to support business planning first, then action, and lastly analysis.

Examine the ways in which your organization supports its various planning functions with information resources. If low or nonexistent, consider shifting resources from support of analysis or action into support for planning.

IS effectiveness and business performance are directly related. We found that companies exhibiting the most satisfaction with the IS-related knowledge of their end users tended to have better business performance. Similarly, companies in which there was high satisfaction with the information being provided by the information systems exhibited higher levels of business performance. And finally, companies satisfied with the support IS had provided to connecting the firm to its markets, customers and suppliers also performed better than others.

These findings suggest that as a manager you should first examine how knowledgeable are the non-IS professionals who use information technology in their jobs. Appropriate training should be implemented if this knowledge is low. Next, you should measure how satisfied the various members of your organization are with the information IS is giving them. If necessary, you should take steps to raise this satisfaction level. Also, you should examine opportunities for connecting your organization to its customers and suppliers using information technology, such as electronic data interchange.

It is critical that an organization's IS resources be deployed so as to best support the organization's strategic orientation. But how do you do this?

Many of today's organizations are moving quickly to downsize their IS operations, shifting more of their applications to networks of personal computers, and ridding themselves of their large computers. The thinking that drives this kind of movement is primarily cost-based: networks of PCs cost much less than large mainframes, although the substantial hidden costs in a PC-network computing environment may temper these economics somewhat. Seldom do companies consider these changes based on the impact they will have on IS strategic alignment. The problem is that cost reductions can be seen to impact a company's bottom line directly; until now, achieving improved strategic alignment has been commonly viewed as a good thing, but without a clear bottom-line impact.

Our study shows that there is indeed a strong relationship between good strategic alignment and the firm's bottom line. We cannot say from our data that it is more important to achieve alignment than to reduce costs, but we can say that alignment matters a great deal. Organizations that do not take this into careful consideration in managing their IS functions are missing an important lever for improving their business' performance.

Learning to Use Information Technology for Competitive Advantage

Mary Crossan

Mary Crossan is a professor of strategic management at the Richard Ivey School of Business.

All organizations learn — for better or worse. By understanding how they learn, companies can begin to manage the process to enhance their strategic performance. And using information technology to harness the learning that takes place in your organization can help your company to gain and sustain its competitive advantage.

Organizational learning occurs within and across three levels: individual, group and organization. At the individual level are the competencies and capabilities needed to do one's job. Group-level learning combines individual learning, recognizing that the whole can be greater than the sum of its parts. The organizational level is where learning becomes embedded in the company's non-human artifacts, such as systems, structures, procedures and strategy. Learning at the organization level remains even after individuals leave the company. To ensure that the right things are being learned, organizational learning needs to be connected to the company's strategic orientation. The classic strategic analysis applies: learning must help the organization to meet the competitive challenges in the marketplace.

What has been learned by individuals, groups and the organization makes up a company's intellectual capital. However, this capital needs to be activated before it can be useful.

Effective use of intellectual capital requires a flow between levels. Individuals acquire or generate new knowledge through training, informal learning and job experience. What they learn gets disseminated to groups and to the organization, for example, in the form of new products and processes. In turn, the learning that becomes embedded in the organization guides what individuals do and how they relate to one another. For example, reward systems are a strong feedback mechanism that guides what individuals pay attention to and how they spend their time. Also, organization structures often determine who ends up talking to whom in the organization.

However, companies may be overinvesting in individual learning by failing to put processes and systems in place to ensure the effective flow of that learning throughout the organization. IBM of the 1980s is a classic example. Renowned for developing its employees, IBM didn't have the capacity to absorb the new knowledge individuals were bringing into the company. The result: employees, who grew frustrated at not being able to use their knowledge, left in droves, with their expertise.

The value of managing the development of intellectual capital is clear; the role that information technology plays, less clear. Unfortunately, many IT specialists have been mistakenly equating data with information, information with knowledge and knowledge with learning. Data are merely bits and bytes, information is meaningfully organized data, and knowledge is useful information. And organizational learning is the overall process where knowledge is made part of the company's strategic thrust. Without organizational learning, not only are data and information essentially valueless, but knowledge is as well.

IT as a Support to Organizational Learning

Integrating IT, strategy and human resource management is an absolute prerequisite for effective organizational learning. You need to know first which knowledge has value — the strategic dimension — and how people learn best — human resources management — before designing systems that facilitate organizational learning.

IT plays two critical roles in organizational learning. First, it provides the infrastructure for the learning flow between individuals, groups and the organization. Second, IT often acts as a storehouse for individual and group learning that becomes embedded in the organization's databases. Some organizations may use products like Lotus Notes as a forum for discussing new ideas and sharing knowledge. But the reality of organizational learning is that taking new ideas, developing a shared understanding of them, and then embedding them in products, systems and procedures begins with an informal, typically person-to-person process. There is no shortcut. Information technology should aid the flow of learning and not be imposed as a structure in which learning is forced to fit. Interestingly, Xerox discovered that its copier repair people are better at developing and sharing their knowledge when they are trading "war stories" over coffee — informal, but effective. The well-known example of 3M's development of the Post-it™ Note underscores another informal, and highly successful, knowledge flow of an idea from the individual to the organization.

Many organizations have latched onto IT as a means of distributing knowledge or enhancing the flow of learning from individuals and groups to the organization. However, whether individuals are learning from that data flow is another question. Unfortunately, the data does flow, but learning is often only assumed to have occurred.

Consulting firms have been grappling with the challenge of capturing and sharing the learning within their own organizations. Many have done so by emphasizing IT as the primary mechanism for learning. Consultants are required to codify and share their learning. This, of course, assumes that the learning can be codified, shared, understood and acted upon by someone else. The shortcomings of this approach are highlighted by a recent discussion with a consultant who expressed great frustration at the firm's over-reliance on shared learning through IT. The consultant, who had developed expertise in one area, had been called upon by another consultant to e-mail the procedure manual on how to engage a client in a visioning process. The frustrated consultant expressed the view that the firm had lost sight of how such expertise had been, and should be, developed. Clearly, it wasn't simply by the flow of bits and bytes through a technology pipeline.

Consider the difference between a technology-driven system designed to capture and disseminate knowledge, and a mentoring system that is largely dependent upon human interaction as a means to develop and share expertise. The strengths of one system are the weaknesses of the other. A technology-based system is not people-dependent and hence remains largely intact even when individuals leave. However, to transfer knowledge it must be codified, and there-fore tacit knowledge, which is non-codifiable, cannot be captured by such a system. The consultant's frustration described above arose largely because of the lack of recognition of the importance of tacit, non-codified knowledge as the true basis of expertise rather than a codified procedure manual. In contrast, a mentoring system provides for the transfer of all forms of knowledge and expertise, yet is entirely dependent upon the people involved for that transfer to occur.

Few managers think of mentoring as an alternative to expert systems. Yet both are simply systems for transferring knowledge. Assigning new employees to learn through informal interaction with more experienced people may take time, but the learning is arguably richer and the experience more rewarding. The fact is, IT solutions to organizational learning problems are not always the best available.

Consulting firms are being singled out here, as they are, to a large extent, setting the knowledge management agenda given their own demands in this area. However, they may be losing sight of the fact that knowledge is only part of the equation — individuals need to be able to act on that knowledge. Understanding the knowledge-action link and the stocks and flows of learning is what organiza-tional learning is all about. Consulting firms have the power to do much good. But if they place too much stress on technology and ignore the behavioral aspects of organizational learning, they can also do much harm.

IT can be useful in the flow of learning from individuals to the orga-nization. Indeed, many cases prove this. For example, General Electric has used IT to capture the ongoing learning it generates in the process of troubleshooting problems customers are having with appliances. But although IT can be useful, it is not always the answer. It has the allure of being a quick fix to the challenges of organizational learning.

Technology may have a greater role to play in facilitating learning flows from the organization to the individual. As storehouses of learning at the organizational level, databases of customer, competitive or perhaps financial data are important depositories of learning. And these data are often meaningfully organized to provide valuable information that can be distributed to individuals and groups in a timely fashion. But many IT systems ignore critical human resources issues, such as how to motivate employees to use and learn from such systems. Or they ignore strategic issues, such as the type of information that needs to be communicated. In addition, there is a tendency to over rely on IT in the decision-making process, which can atrophy an individual's capability to make sound judgments.

Gaining and Sustaining Competitive Advantage

A more significant problem with IT systems is that they can hardly generate a sustainable competitive advantage given they are so easily imitable — once knowledge is codified, it can be leaked to a competitor. Clearly, there are cases where IT and associated databases provide a competitive advantage, as American Airlines found with its Sabre reservation system. While companies want to maximize learning within the organization, they also need to retain competitive advantage by minimizing learning across organizations. Of course there are some exceptions, such as the use of IT to facilitate information flow between a company and its suppliers, for example. The challenge is to facilitate the learning through IT without compromising a company's competitive position.

It is the tacit knowledge that is difficult to codify and hence ill suited to transfer through technology that often provides the basis for competitive advantage. The point is, if it is easy, it is probably easy to replicate. Whereas, effective organizational learning, because of its complexity, is difficult to replicate.

IT can facilitate organizational learning, but it is not a shortcut to transferring expertise. On the one hand, codifying knowledge enables companies to retain something when individuals leave. On the other hand, this practice can result in potential leaks to a competitor. An effective IT system must support and transfer learning throughout the organization in a way that allows enhanced learning to occur, and at the same time allow a company to protect its most valuable resource.

The Rise of Digital Business: Electronic Commerce Is Where the Opportunities Are

Sid L. Huff

Sid L. Huff is a professor of management science and information systems at the Richard Ivey School of Business and the holder of the Hewlett-Packard Chair in Information Technology Management.

Something new and big is happening with information technology (IT) today. No longer just a support mechanism for data processing or information systems, IT is now becoming the very medium of business. How many people regularly used electronic mail to communicate with business associates in other companies five years ago? Who had even heard of a web page three years ago? And before 1995, how many people had ever transacted business using their personal computers? The answer to all these questions is, of course, almost nobody. This paradigm shift is occurring with incredible speed, largely due to the emergence of the Internet, and specifically the World Wide Web, during the last five years. The growth in the awareness and use of the Internet may well be seen by future historians as the most incredible technology story of all time.

During the past three years, the web has become the backbone for global electronic commerce. The creation and growth of thousands of Internet service provider companies (ISPs) have brought access to the Internet within local-phone-call reach of most people in developed countries. Developing nations are also moving quickly to provide their citizenry with access to the Internet — anyone with a PC and a telephone in Ulaanbataar, Mongolia's capital, can acquire an Internet account through Datacom Mongolia, that country's first ISP. Worldwide spending on Internet and related technologies will reach almost US$100 billion in the year 2000 — five times higher than the US$19 billion spent in 1996, according to the International Data Corporation.

The first use of the web for electronic commerce was simple advertising. In fact, many firms have not progressed much beyond putting their "home page" on the web to advertise their products or services to anyone who cares to access their site. But if the web merely provided a new advertising medium, much of the excitement that surrounds it would have died down by now. After all, for a company that already advertises in print, or on television, radio or billboards, the web is just another outlet. But the Internet has continued to grow exponentially and offers opportunities to electronic commerce on an unimaginable scale.

Superior Information Provision

Even if you choose to go no further with the web than providing information about your company and its products or services, the web offers several opportunities not available through other media. First, you can provide more information, but organize it in a way that allows visitors to access only what they are interested in, to skim or to otherwise interact with your site as they wish. You can update online information more frequently and easily than if it were being provided in other forms. You can provide information in many ways, including static text, images, "live" demonstrations, and voice and video clips. You can go one step further and gather data and opinions from inquirers. Further, you can provide dynamic information to such visitors by connecting your web site into your back-office information systems. If I want to know where the FedEx package I sent yesterday afternoon is right now, I can connect to the FedEx web site, enter my shipping code, and find out exactly where it is and when it should arrive at its destination.

Intranet Opportunities

An intranet is simply a network using Internet standards and infrastructure that is maintained inside your company and is walled off from the outside Internet. This works especially well for a company with widely dispersed operational sites. A company's portion of the global Internet can be used almost as if it were the firm's own proprietary network system; an intranet can provide online access to company documents — for example, training manuals or company reports — thereby saving paper and distribution costs, and avoiding the use of obsolete information.

Extranet Opportunities

An extranet — the logical extension of an intranet — extends, in a limited way, beyond the boundary of your own organization to include specific business partners, such as suppliers, clients, business partners or even competitors. The Internet network makes creating an extranet much simpler than a more traditional proprietary company-to-company or multicompany network. Applications that run on the extranet can range from simple information sharing to more sophisticated real-time inquiries or even transaction data exchanges.

Internet-Based Selling

CDnow, "the world's largest music store," and a rapidly growing number of other companies have built their businesses completely on the Internet. While you may not wish to run your entire business over the Internet, you might want to consider executing a part of it this way — if for no other reason than to get a foot in the door. Most observers agree that retail commerce over the Internet is where the largest opportunities lie.

Stepping up to Internet selling is easy. Many software tools are available to help you construct and maintain a site that supports customer purchases. In addition, the number of trained webmasters who can assist you is growing very rapidly.

Electronic Financial Transactions

The Internet can be used for financial transactions, such as disbursements and payments. Here things start getting more challenging — though not for long. Although the dominant form of payment over the Internet is the credit card, security concerns have limited the acceptance of this practice. Advances in security and encryption are coming fast, and knowledgeable people argue that the Internet is already a far more secure place to use your credit card than the typical restaurant. Nevertheless, as long as people think the Internet is unsafe for financial transactions, they will be slow to use it in this way.

The widespread adoption of "digital money" — smart cards, electronic checks, digital "coins," or the use of trusted third parties — may soon solve this security issue. A problem with credit card–based Internet payments today is that the associated transaction fees make them non-viable for very small purchases. The successful digital money solution must be able to handle such micro-transactions cost-effectively. Once that occurs, many Internet information providers who give their service away for free today will begin to charge a small, but in total very significant, fee for their use.

Integrated Supply Chain Management

Finally, you can start to develop end-to-end electronic relationships within your industry. The main objective of this concept is to streamline the movement of manufactured goods from raw material sources to the final customer's hands, by providing early warning about supply-and-demand fluctuations, parts and inventory status, and shipments from one end of the integrated supply chain to the other. In effect, the various firms making up the supply chain become members of a "virtual community," functioning as a coordinated, extended team to improve the business processes across several cooperating organizations.

Companies are no longer simply trying to eke out basic efficiency improvements with supply chain management; rather, they are focusing more on outcomes, such as revenue growth and improved customer service, as ways of differentiating themselves from their competition.

To see the benefits of superior supply chain management, one need look no further than the success experienced by Michael Dell and Dell Computer Corporation. The company sells computers directly to end users; doesn't manufacture, but rather assembles to order; uses the Internet very effectively throughout its operations; and is approaching $10 billion in sales.

Getting There from Here

Unquestionably, the Internet holds many compelling features. However, getting there from here holds many challenges, the most worrisome of which is security. People seem to have a greater concern when they cannot actually see the person with whom they are transacting. Solving the security problem is arguably the most pressing challenge of Internet commerce.

Another challenge revolves around the fact that the Internet is a very busy place today, so busy that some people have started calling it the "world wide wait." The Internet's infrastructure has not kept up with the incredible growth in usage over the past three years. Because nobody really "owns" the Internet, people have no place to go to demand better service. It is often impossible to determine exactly the source of bottlenecks. But the general nature of the problem is clear: insufficient bandwidth (the capacity for transmitting data).

New approaches are being tried for increasing the bandwidth of the links between individual homes and their Internet service providers — including cable modems from the cable television providers, and something called an asynchronous digital subscriber line (ADSL) from the telephone companies. Several organizations — mainly in the United States — are experimenting with new technology for reconstructing the Internet's "backbone." These experiments are aimed at creating an "Internet 2" that will have the bandwidth and processing capacity to handle future demands.

Perhaps the greatest challenge of all concerns not technology, but people. At the day's end it is individuals who have to decide to adopt Internet commerce if the widely touted visions are to become reality. Close to 40 percent of North American homes are already Internet-capable, and this is expected to exceed 50 percent by the year 2000. So far, only a very small percentage of these households have actually purchased something through the Internet.

Of course, retail purchases are just one aspect of electronic commerce. Indeed, the company-to-company use of the Internet has proceeded much more rapidly than has retail use. Nonetheless, retail commerce through the Internet is the most critical piece, because that is where millions of potential consumers await.

Those close to the action of Internet commerce say that it is not a matter of if, but when, widespread consumer adoption of Internet commerce takes place. Time will tell — and considering that Internet time progresses roughly 10 times faster than regular time — we shouldn't have to wait long to find out.

Growing Smart Businesses Takes "Smart" Capital

Rick Norland

*Rick Norland is a founding part-
ner in Thorington Corporation,
an investment banking firm serving emerging, advanced-technology
companies. He holds an MBA
from the Richard Ivey School of
Business and is a member of the
steering committee to Ivey's Institute for Entrepreneurship, Innovation and Growth.*

The stars in our information technology industry
have at least one thing in common with
hundreds of other aspiring advanced-technology
ventures — they started small. Launching an information technology (IT) company typically requires no
more than a couple of entrepreneurs with a great idea
— an innovation hot from the research and development lab. Intel began this way. So did Newbridge,
Cognos, Corel, Mitel and an array of other successful
companies throughout Silicon Valley North.

Getting started is relatively easy. The hard part can be growing the business and finding the resources appropriate for each stage in the company's growth. This is a challenge for any business, but in the highly competitive, superaccelerated information technology sector, managing growth while constantly moving is particularly complex.

One of the toughest issues for young, fast-growing companies is finding capital. The search for investors is frequently a task outside the core competency of an IT startup. As such, it can steal time and attention from critical business development concerns, such as finding a distribution channel, meeting a release date and securing a beta-test site.

Finding capital is also a high-risk process fraught with questions and make-or-break decisions. Should I take the company public now? Can I find a private placement and still maintain control of the business? Where are the angel investors when you need them? What kind of return do they expect?

Although each enterprise is different, and investors' interest in the industry itself shifts every day, a few rules of thumb can guide IT companies seeking to manage and fund their growth.

First, understand where you are in the growth cycle of your product, and develop an appropriate financing strategy. In a dynamic industry such as IT, this may not be as easy as it sounds. A variety of considerations — including gross revenue, profit or profit projections and product cycles — will assist you in locating your company on the growth curve. This, along with financial projections to indicate your capital requirements, will help to determine the right financing strategy.

Second, do everything you can to build the valuation of your company before you start seeking investment. This sounds intuitive, but it's frequently overlooked. Company A, whose primary asset is a "killer" application software, may achieve a specific valuation. Company B, with the same piece of software plus a superb marketing strategy and a board of directors with considerable "bench strength," may be valued at twice as much. By paying attention to business basics you can increase the value assigned to your company. And the higher your company's valuation, the less equity and control you'll have to surrender to investors.

Third, know the difference between capital and "smart" capital. It's a mistake, particularly in IT, to assume that all capital is created equal. Seek investment sources that will bring strategic value to your

Matching Financial Requirements and Sources with Growth Stage

	Up to $100,000	$100,000 – $500,000	$500,000 – $1 million	$1 million	$2 million	$5 million	> $15 million
	Seed Stage	Early Stage	Startup Stage	Distribution Stage	Sales Stage	Profit Stage	Initial Public Offering / Minimum 3 years of profits
	The project moves from concept to working model to engineering prototype	Production prototypes are produced	The final product is produced	Product is distributed and sales begin	Sales reach a breakeven point	Product is now successful	Public Markets
Sources of Funds	Personal Savings, Friends and Government programs	Active Informal Investors	Active Informal Investors	Corporate/Strategic Alliance	Venture Capitalists	Institutional Private Placement	

enterprise, well beyond the simple cash itself. If you're a multimedia company, for example, you can find corporate investors or venture capital firms with previous investments in multimedia. What they've learned may be of value to your company, and their portfolios may contain potential alliances with marketing channel members, complementary technologies and key suppliers or customers. An investor of this nature will help grow your business in ways a purely financial investor cannot.

Last, get help if you need it. Planning a financing strategy is risky business. A mistake can result in significant dilution to the current shareholders, even a change in control.

Joining the Millions Already on the Net

Michael Parent

Michael Parent is a professor of management information systems at the Richard Ivey School of Business.

Network Wizards of Menlo Park, California, recently announced results of the latest semi-official count of Internet connections. As of July 1997, 19.5 million host systems were connected to the Net. Of these, 4.5 million are in what is referred to the .com domain, reserved for private companies. The .com domain is the fastest-growing sector of Internet connections, with an annual growth rate of 52 percent. More than 600,000 new .com hosts went online in the first six months of that year. In other words, companies are flocking to the Internet. The question is, are they percipient pioneers or merely lemmings?

The Net is a compelling phenomenon. Many managers, dazzled by the possibilities, are under enormous pressure to be part of it. They fear that somehow they'll lose an important competitive edge if their companies don't have a presence on the World Wide Web — right now. In the rush, they sometimes fail to ask the important question: "What business benefits can the Internet deliver to my company?"

No general answer exists; it depends on the company and the application. The only thing you can say — and it could be said about any corporate investment — is that managers should measure costs against expected benefits carefully. Unfortunately, in the current information technology environment, it seems unlikely many will do this.

Too many technology investment decisions are made without a full and clear understanding of their impact. This may be one reason why the biggest area for investment by business continues to be information technology and telecom systems. The Conference Board of Canada indicates that businesses invested a total of $22.2 billion in IT and telecom in 1986. By 1992, the figure had jumped to $47.9 billion. And this is despite the compelling evidence that IT spending does not translate into increased productivity as it was supposed to do.

Economists tell us that in the seven richest nations, productivity growth has taken a nosedive in the past 30 years — from 4.5 percent in the 1960s to 1.5 percent in recent years. And this, paradoxically, during a period when investment in IT was burgeoning.

Many explanations have been offered as to why this "productivity paradox," but the simplest — that corporations have overspent on IT — seems the most plausible. Part of the problem is a too-easy acceptance by managers that it is inevitable some of their IT spending will be wasted. Many banks, for example, are currently investing in several different online banking technologies — one, of course, being the Internet — despite the fact that they know that much of the investment will be scrapped when one technology establishes dominance.

Their dilemma is neatly summed up in the apocryphal story of the CEO who confessed he knew half his IT budget was being wasted — he just didn't know which half.

The problem is, executives still don't know how to accurately measure the impact of much of the technology in which they invest — and maybe never will know. It's easy enough to measure the benefits of transactional systems, but if a company implements systems to enhance executive decision-making, for example, how do you measure that?

The climate of uncertainty about the value of technology sometimes produces shockingly poor investment decisions. In one recent federal government project, the proposal from the winning contractor estimated the price for software development at $250 million. Midway through the project, the supplier bumped the figure to $365 million.

To countenance this kind of overspending is simply not rational decision-making — and yet it's common. Savvy executives routinely multiply any estimate for IT services by a factor of two and are delighted if the overbudget factor ends up being only 1.5. Clearly, any manager who wants to make a rational evaluation of proposed investments in the Internet should keep the productivity paradox in mind.

Despite this potential paradox, the Internet does have great potential as a business tool. It can be harnessed as a kind of extended — and much less expensive — alternative to groupware tools such as Lotus Notes, providing managers and professionals a forum in which to exchange ideas and knowledge. Internet surfers already use Usenet groups in much the same way that corporate employees use Lotus Notes discussion threads.

The Net can also function as an informal and far-reaching executive information system. A large part of many executives' jobs involves scanning the business environment. It may now be easier for them to find out what their competitors are doing by going to their web sites than by subscribing to expensive newspaper and magazine clipping services.

But using the Internet as a tool for promoting a company and its products and selling these online remains problematic for two reasons. First, establishing and managing a presence on the web is far from painless. It requires significant initial and ongoing investments in people and IT infrastructure, typically at least a webmaster and a marketing team. And it's not enough just to mount some pages and leave them there. If you want web surfers to come back repeatedly, you have to update continually. Companies that get into it soon discover that a web site can seem like a bottomless pit into which they must keep pouring money. Second, because of the fantastic growth of the World Wide Web, especially among companies establishing web sites, it's difficult to differentiate your company in cyberspace on "look and feel" alone. Plus, since the web is primarily a pull medium, your customers have to choose to come to your site.

Of course, there are ways to overcome these problems. You can place banner ads on web pages that receive a lot of user "traffic," for example. One company decided the best way to get noticed on the web was to make sure its pages showed up among the first 10 "hits" in lists generated by search engines. Its web site developers set about learning how to compose pages the search engines would find first. This turned out to be a painstaking process of trial and error.

It's true that there are isolated success stories of using the Internet to obtain customer transactions. For example, Amazon Books has created an online bookstore, Amazon.com, that allows book lovers to browse almost a million titles. But the fact that the evidence is so anecdotal is in itself suspicious. If you struck pay dirt on the web, would you want to tell others how you did it?

Impressive statistics on the growth of Internet commerce should also be viewed with caution. IBM vice-president Mark Greene told an Internet World conference audience in early 1997 that world-wide Internet commerce would hit US$200 billion a year in transactions by the decade's end. You should determine if such information is veri-fied by research or is intended to motivate customers to see the need to purchase Internet technology.

But the fundamental question all managers should be asking is, "Where is the competitive advantage in having a web presence when 4.5 million companies around the world are already there before me?" The answer, I believe, is nowhere. The web will face a situation simi-lar to that faced by automated banking machines and bank machine networks. They became table stakes in the game of banking — if you didn't "ante up" with your own ABMs and if you didn't connect them to the networks, then you couldn't play. The result was that no one bank ended up with any lasting competitive advantage.

So, perhaps the question managers should be asking is not, "How can I grab a competitive advantage for my company by establishing a presence on the web?" but rather, "How long can I delay before I have to ante up?"

Getting Technology-Intensive Products to Market

Adrian Ryans,
Roger More, Don Barclay
and Terry Deutscher

Adrian Ryans, Roger More, Don Barclay and Terry Deutscher are professors of marketing at the Richard Ivey School of Business. This article is adapted from the introductory chapter of their upcoming book Winning Market Leadership in Technology-Intensive Markets *(forthcoming).*

When Gil Amelio became the CEO of Apple Computer in February 1996, he faced a massive strategic market planning challenge. Although many users no longer saw Apple's Macintosh user interface as being significantly better than Microsoft's Windows 95 interface, Apple's prices remained higher than those of other personal computers. In the still-growing PC market, its global market share was declining rapidly. Apple's market leadership was no longer clear and the company was losing money.

Mr. Amelio faced some very tough choices. Should Apple put more emphasis on "cheap," more competitively priced Macs? Should it be more aggressive in licensing the Mac operating system to other manufacturers? Should Apple focus on those market segments where it historically had a very strong following, or should it emphasize emerging markets? Mr. Amelio and his team had to resolve some tough questions quickly if Apple was to be saved. In the view of Apple's board of directors, Mr. Amelio did not make the tough choices quickly enough, and he resigned from Apple in July 1997.

Apple isn't an isolated case. Managers in technology-intensive businesses grapple with an overwhelming number of challenging planning issues. But by using a systematic process that allows them to consider all major factors influencing their difficult choices, they can focus on winning market leadership.

Strategic market planning for technology-intensive businesses is made particularly challenging due to the environment in which they operate:

- High-tech industries often have complex market chains, with many organizations having to be effectively coordinated to produce the solutions that end users want.
- Because their markets are so turbulent, high-tech businesses must continually question their roles in customer value creation. Also, changes in technology or markets can bring significant discontinuities, which can provide opportunities to topple the current market leaders. For example, in the 1960s and 1970s, IBM was unable to transfer its leadership position in mainframes to the emerging minicomputer market. Digital Equipment Corporation (DEC) and Hewlett-Packard Company emerged as the leaders in what became a high-growth market segment.
- New ways of providing a particular functionality to a customer group are continually emerging, sometimes providing products with dramatically improved price/performance. In the mid-1980s, Aldus Corporation successfully created the desktop publishing market with its software product Page-Maker. But within a few years, the once-clear boundary

around the desktop publishing market was blurred as word processing packages, such as WordPerfect and Word, added more desktop publishing features to their programs.

- Technology-intensive industries require large investments to develop new technologies and new products, and given the short life cycles of such products, the only way to achieve the large volumes needed to recoup these investments is to aggressively sell the product globally. Managers face all the problems associated with dealing with foreign markets.

Winning Market Leadership: An Integrated Approach

Overcoming these problems requires strategic market planning — selecting and creating the business opportunities you will pursue, and developing the marketing plans to make you a leader in your targeted markets.

Since it is not possible in technology-intensive businesses to divorce technology decisions from marketing decisions, and since employees at all levels of the organization will be expected to implement the plan, the process requires multifunctional and multilevel teams. The process emphasizes selecting the right set of market opportunities — a challenge in many technology-intensive markets, which may have hundreds of opportunities. The process places heavy emphasis on market chains, on understanding the competitive environment and on managing multiple, shifting relationships.

Define the Business Arena

The first step in the planning process is to identify the broad business arena you will be targeting. Give each arena of opportunity a business definition along four major dimensions:

- potential customer segments that could be served;
- potential applications or functionality that could be provided to these customers;
- possible technologies and capabilities that could be used to create the applications or functionality; and

- possible role for your organization in providing the value to the customer versus the roles of others in the market chain.

At this stage, keep all decisions tentative — you may reconsider and change them as you move through the planning process.

Identify Attractive Opportunities

Sometimes, an opportunity will present itself — a current customer will bring a new need to your attention or your organization's scientists or engineers may have a technological breakthrough. Other times, you may be actively searching for new opportunities if your current ones are not meeting your revenue or earnings targets. Whatever the case, you need to acquire an in-depth understanding of the opportunities in the arena selected.

An important early step in identifying attractive opportunities involves thoroughly segmenting the market. This starts the development of an in-depth understanding of the applications or functionality customers require, the technologies that might be used to deliver the application and the value-added required from the market chain involved.

Next, determine the potential profitability of serving particular market segments. If the market and competitive forces are so negative that no company serving this market segment is likely to be profitable, then you might eliminate this market segment from further consideration. But maybe not; in 1996, Sony Corporation, a leader in consumer electronics, announced its entry into the desktop PC market, despite the fact that few companies were making money in this market by that time. Sometimes, management can see a way to change a segment's dynamics or feels that, for strategic reasons, it has to have a presence in the segment. Sony clearly felt that the potential convergence of the home computer and home entertainment markets made it essential that it develop a strong presence in the home computer market.

As you conduct your analysis, watch for market segments that may allow you to drive the market by adopting a radically different strategy. Such opportunities arise when major discontinuities occur in a market, such as a technology breakthrough or deregulation.

Once your planning team has identified opportunities that look attractive, it — or generally, a smaller, cross-functional team — can then take these opportunities, either individually or as a group, through the next three steps of the process.

Understand the Market

Lay out the actual and potential market chains that could supply the targeted end users with the proposed product or service. This visual representation, extending from major suppliers of raw materials for the product through to your distribution channels, is one to which your planning team will return often.

Next, develop an appreciation of buyer behavior in the potential target segments. If customers' needs are being met by other suppliers, determine what will influence the target customers to switch to your product.

You also need to understand the market chain, including the decision-making units that will be involved, the members' buying criteria and the likely buying process they will go through. In some cases, major barriers to adopting the proposed product or service may surface, resulting in this opportunity being dropped.

Assess Resources and Core Capabilities

After looking at the external marketplace, assess the available internal resources (including financial resources, technology platforms, intellectual capital, manufacturing capacity and brand equity) and capabilities (including skills and knowledge). Again, the internal situation may be such that you abandon the opportunity.

Understand the Competitive Environment

Although a competitive analysis is a key part of the analysis of the external environment, it is best done after reviewing your company's resources and capabilities — you are always in a better position to assess competitors if you have carefully looked at your own position first.

Any competitive analysis has two fundamental purposes: to determine if winning a profitable position in a particular market opportunity is likely, and to develop the strategy and tactics that will allow you to achieve that winning position. Clearly, you need to assess the resources and capabilities of your potential competitors not only in an absolute sense, but also relative to your resources and capabilities.

To conduct the competitive analysis, first identify the actual, potential and indirect competitors your organization will face. The indirect competitors are simply the companies that use a different technology to meet the same functional need of the customer. If your planning team did a good job of its market forces analysis when it was assessing the opportunity's attractiveness, this step should be straightforward.

Next, determine how each competitor competes, their current and likely future performances, and what drivers underlie their business strategies. Sometimes changes in key executives, such as a new CEO, can signal that a major shift in strategy is imminent. For example, when George Fisher became Eastman Kodak's CEO in 1993, he sold all of Kodak's businesses that were unrelated to imaging, and placed Kodak's embryonic digital imaging businesses in a separate business unit from its traditional silver halide photography businesses. This increased focus on electronic imaging was an important development for both competitors and complementors in digital imaging.

As a final step in a competitive analysis, consider the implications for the opportunity being evaluated. What is this competitor likely to do next? What are this competitor's areas of weakness or vulnerability that you could exploit? How is this competitor likely to react if you do X, Y or Z? What has your planning team learned that could make your organization a stronger, more effective competitor?

Strategic Thinking and Choices

For each individual opportunity, two common strategic issues arise. The first addresses winning, and involves selecting the best strategy for taking advantage of the opportunity. Based on the analysis your planning team has done, can it develop a strategy that will allow the organization to achieve a leadership position in the opportunity? The second issue involves deciding whether or not this is an opportunity that should be pursued. What will it be worth to win? Is the market opportunity attractive enough and is the strategy powerful enough to generate a level of profitability that will meet your financial targets?

Or if not, are there compelling reasons to proceed? For example, it might make it easier to seize other opportunities that promise to be highly profitable. This was probably Sony's motivation for entering the PC business.

When you consider the entire portfolio of opportunities, strategic issues often arise as to how well the opportunities fit with each other — do synergies exist within the portfolio, such as leveraging on a common technology or market chain? Also ask if the strategies for the various opportunities are reasonably consistent. For example, a strategy based on product leadership for one product line is unlikely to be workable with a strategy of cost leadership for a related line.

Perhaps the most challenging aspect of any strategic thinking process is making the hard choices between the opportunities. But any good planning process should select the few truly attractive opportunities, concentrate the resources on these opportunities and develop a leadership position in them.

By now, most key decisions will have been made, and generally, the initiative returns to the team that did the analysis of the opportunity. They will finalize the strategy and build the implementation plan.

Plan Key Relationships

In many technology-intensive industries, developing and managing the relationships between your organization and the market chain is crucial for success. In addition, important relationships may need to be developed with individuals or organizations outside the market chain — perhaps a company with a complementary product or service that will enhance your offering.

Complete the Winning Strategy

To complete the winning strategy, attend to pricing and marketing communications. Both activities can help create the economic incentive for others in the market chain to work with you rather than with your competitors. Your strategy must allow all key players in the market chain to achieve their business and personal objectives by working with you.

Understand the Profit Dynamic

A more refined profitability analysis is possible now that you have a detailed understanding of the complete marketing strategy and the associated costs. Develop a detailed financial model for each opportunity that has reached this stage in the planning process. This analysis may suggest modifications to the strategy that may enhance the opportunity's overall profitability.

Implement Strategy

Finally, you are ready to implement the strategic market plan. No matter how good a strategy is, ineffectively implementing it will ensure failure. One way to ensure it is done right is to have the people who will play key roles in the implementation heavily involved in — and committed to — the strategy. They will then contribute to the strategy's development, understand the rationale for particular choices and be able to make the many minor adjustments in strategy needed as the theory behind the strategy hits the shifting reality of the marketplace.

Strategic market planning requires the ideas and energy from all of a company's major functional units. As the plan comes together, finalize the supporting functional strategies in such areas as R&D, purchasing, manufacturing and logistics.

In technology-intensive businesses, the transition from strategy development to implementation is seldom smooth; the environment is too fast-moving for such a clear demarcation. Even as you begin the implementation process, the strategy is evolving, which requires adjustments to the implementation process. It is truly an interactive, evolving process.

Technology Acquisitions: Questions from the Directors

Ted White

Ted White, a corporate director of 30 companies and chairman of Tandem Computers Canada, addressed this issue at the recently held Directors Program at the Richard Ivey School of Business.

As major technology initiatives become more critical to ensuring business competitiveness, corporate directors are faced with the challenge of reviewing and approving projects that often involve expenditures of tens of millions of dollars. And all this occurs against a backdrop where there are an increasing number of high-profile technology failures. A 1996 study conducted by the Standish Group International found that 42 percent of corporate information technology projects were abandoned before completion. Further, the bigger the project, the higher the failure rate.

While the challenge of approving technological acquisitions can be difficult for any director, it is especially so for those with no background in technology.

To heighten their comfort level, directors should focus their attention on the process by which management reaches the recommendation as well as on the specifics of the technology proposal.

Asking the right questions will help directors to uncover potential risks in acquisitions, help them to understand the alternatives that were considered by project managers and aid them in evaluating the quality of the staff work that underlies the recommendation.

A series of open-ended questions will assist management in describing to their directors the process used to come to the recommendation. Directors should ask management:

1. to describe the assessment and decision-making process;
2. to state the alternative approaches they considered;
3. to describe the major considerations or factors that influenced their decision;
4. to postulate the worst thing that could happen if they are wrong;
5. to describe the nature of the debate that went on during the evaluation process;
6. to propose how they plan to measure the progress of the project during implementation as well as the benefits to be realized after implementation.

These questions will provide background information that often leads to some closed-ended questions. Closed-ended questions reveal specific details of the process, allowing directors to assess the risk involved. Ask management:

1. Was the decision an easy one? Why or why not?
2. How many different solutions (vendors) did they consider?
3. What were the second and third choices? How close were they? Why did they disqualify them?
4. Did they use a consultant to assist in their decision? Was the consultant's recommendation a strong one? Did he or she have a second choice? What questions or concerns did he or she express?
5. Has anybody else adopted this solution? In our industry? Is it working? Have they talked to their counterpart there?

6. What is the market share of their chosen vendor in this area?
7. What are the risks of dealing with this vendor?
8. Are there relevant standards in this technology space?
9. Does their proposed solution meet these standards?

To determine the real significance of the proposal to the company, directors need to ask a few questions related to timing:

1. Why now?
2. What are the consequences of waiting?
3. What are the consequences of not doing it at all?

To determine the bottom-line benefit of the technology acquisition, ask what the real payoff is. Any payoffs that extend beyond two years in either the elapsed project implementation time or the return on investment should be questioned.

Examining the process that led to management's recommendation is useful in helping directors understand and evaluate any management proposal, especially if the subject matter is unfamiliar to them. Generally, what ensues from a process discussion is often more productive than the exploration of the recommendation's specifics themselves.

III
Marketing Management:
Keeping the Engine Humming

The Evolution of Optimum Dynamic Pricing

Peter C. Bell and Sandy Staples

Peter C. Bell is a professor of management science and information systems at the Richard Ivey School of Business. Sandy Staples is a professor of information systems at the University of Melbourne and a graduate of Ivey's Ph.D. program.

Not long ago, when you planned a trip by air, you were almost guaranteed empty seats next to you on the plane, and you knew what the price of the ticket was going to be before you purchased it. But as a result of American Airlines' pioneering work begun in the early 1980s, the face of airline travel has changed dramatically. Today, most flights leave almost full and fares are no longer one set price. Intense competition has forced other air carriers to follow American's lead. What American Airlines has done to improve efficiency and reduce costs is evolutionary. But what is revolutionary is the concept of optimum dynamic pricing that American developed.

American's pricing objective is to fill seats at maximum revenue. Using "optimum dynamic pricing," seat prices are highly volatile, adjusting often to reflect changing market conditions and inventory. American believes that flying aircraft with high passenger loads is more profitable than flying empty seats — which probably accounts for the demise of high-service, but low-load, carriers.

Optimum dynamic pricing has transformed the airline business and has already spread to many other service industries. Evidence suggests that it's about to have an equally dramatic effect on the retail sector.

Although long considered an important marketing variable, product prices have usually been fixed, with companies living with whatever sales volume these prices generate. Consumers and producers have grown used to products having relatively stable prices. They expect a can of beans to have the same price whether purchased Monday or Wednesday. Of course, some notable exceptions exist, including the stock markets, used cars and gasoline.

Optimum dynamic pricing requires a change in the belief that price is managerially controlled and quantity sold is market controlled. Consider a company that wants to manipulate prices so that sales meet a predetermined volume objective. Wanting to sell 50 units of a product over five days and expecting demand to be even across the five days, it must sell 10 units each day to achieve its objective. On day one, a price of $100 each is posted. At day's end, inventory is checked. If fewer than 10 units have been sold, product price is reduced — the greater the shortfall, the greater the reduction. If more than 10 units have been sold, the price is held or even increased. At the end of day two, the process is repeated. Finally, on day five, a price is posted that will clear the remaining inventory. The 50 units are sold, but management's skill at price-setting and the market determine the revenue received.

Although this example contains nothing revolutionary, such an approach has been able to be implemented only recently. Today, point-of-sale technology gives managers the data needed to monitor product sales and adjust prices frequently to avoid excess inventory situations. Soon technology will allow the price of many products to be adjusted hourly rather than daily.

Firms that practice optimum dynamic pricing see product prices as decision variables that can be manipulated consciously and frequently to enhance profits. This view, together with new technology to calculate optimum prices and to deliver these prices into the marketplace, is revolutionizing markets and the manner in which firms compete. The effective optimum dynamic pricer is emerging as a formidable competitor.

What is an "optimum price"? Consider a company with 500 cakes to sell in one day, and cakes unsold by day's end are waste. Since the product is "on hand," the purchase cost is "sunk." Therefore, the company should set a price that maximizes revenue from sales. The optimum price can be computed if a key component is known — the product's demand curve. The demand curve can be estimated from data on product prices and quantities sold. A company that has dynamically priced several thousand products for a few years will have a vast database to use in estimating its demand curves, and will have developed the skills to derive these curves efficiently and effectively.

Assume that our cake company faces a demand curve that can be approximated by Price = 12 − 0.01 × Quantity Sold. The problem, known as a "constrained optimization" problem, is finding the price that maximizes revenue while selling 500 or fewer units. This solution is to set the price at $7 (12 − 0.01 × 500), which by generating a demand for 500 units, clears out inventory and achieves a maximum revenue of $3,500.

Optimum pricing becomes "dynamic" when this pricing concept is extended to products that have a shelf life of more than one period — the product's price is optimized each period. A series of prices is set, aimed at maximizing sales revenue while planning that no inventory remains at the end of the product's life.

Imagine that a store sells bread with a shelf life of five selling days and that product price may only be changed overnight. The dynamic pricing problem on selling day one is to choose a price for each of the five days such that the total sales revenue is maximized. To solve this problem, the demand curve for each day is needed. If each demand curve is the same each day, the price will remain static. Otherwise, prices in periods of higher demand will be higher.

At the end of day one, the day's sales data are used to revise the estimated demand curves for days two through five, and then the four prices for the four remaining periods are recalculated. This process of revising demand curve estimates and then reassessing price levels based on the remaining stock is repeated each day in the selling period.

Under pure dynamic pricing, prices may go up or down from one day to the next depending on whether sales were higher or lower than expected. However, if raising prices is unacceptable, constraints can be added to ensure that prices remain stable or fall. But firms that impose such constraints will see reduced revenues compared with firms that do not.

Since each period that a dynamic price is set produces a data point that can be used to estimate a new family of demand curves, established dynamic pricers gain a competitive advantage. They can extract increasingly accurate estimates of demand curves that take into account competitors' prices, day-of-the-week, week-of-the-month, season-of-the-year and even time-of-day. As a result, a product's price can be changed weekly, daily or even hourly. But without appropriate technology, these calculated prices cannot reach the marketplace.

To implement dynamic pricing successfully, a firm must have the technology to perform three critical tasks. First, the firm must be able to acquire sales data quickly enough to be able to recompute prices. Second, it must have the technology necessary to compute the optimum prices. And third, it must have the technology to deliver new and variable prices to the marketplace.

The data requirements to drive dynamic pricing can be massive. Each period, the firm must know the prices and sales of all its products, as well as other useful data that affects sales, such as competitors' prices and even the weather. The speed of data acquisition determines how often prices can be changed.

Computing each product's optimum price requires access to software that can determine the set of prices that maximize revenue over the product's life while satisfying inventory, price and demand constraints. Such calculations can be large and complex. For example, a firm with 50,000 products, each with a shelf life of 90 days, has to determine some 4,500,000 revenue-maximizing prices daily. Additional algorithms are needed for developing demand curves and formulating the mathematical programing to permit solutions that are efficient.

Next, the dynamic pricer must be able to communicate new prices back to the marketplace in real time. This generally requires some form of information technology (such as American Airlines' SABRE system) that makes product prices accessible to the prospective buyer electronically.

The Management Challenge

Although today's fast and affordable computers put optimum dynamic pricing within reach, significant human expertise is required to set up these programs — teams of up to 30 management scientists for larger applications. Management of such teams can be complex.

Optimum dynamic pricing presents additional management challenges. Managers must overcome the prospect of losing control over pricing to a computer — the data show that dynamic pricing systems often pick up and react to data more quickly and effectively than humans. Since prices change so quickly, managers must also deal with the possible inability to feature price in advertising.

How customers will react to dynamic prices remains uncertain. People buying equities or used cars rarely complain about changing prices, but many consumers become incensed when discussing varying gasoline prices. How will the person who bought jeans Monday react if the same jeans in the same store are cheaper Tuesday? Firms that can communicate the overall positive impact of dynamic pricing to their customers will be the big winners.

But customers may have other concerns. For example, refund policies will need to be evaluated. Under dynamic pricing, a customer who bought a product at a high price yesterday must be persuaded not to exchange it for the same product at today's lower price. To address such issues in the airline industry, carriers have introduced fees for changing tickets, apparently without major resistance from their customers.

The greatest management challenge most firms will face involves determining whether their competition has implemented optimum dynamic pricing, and if so, what is an appropriate competitive response. The task of monitoring competitors' prices may be complex and costly, particularly if their prices change frequently. Even if monitoring is possible, a "price follower" strategy is a recipe for disaster since the price follower's different inventory levels will lead to situations where it is out of stock or has product surpluses. However, attempting to set a price and hold it is no more likely to be successful, since the dynamic pricer is taking account of the competitor's pricing behavior through observed sales and the nature of the algorithms.

Since perishable products must be sold before they become worthless, setting prices to maximize revenue is logical profit-maximizing behavior. Although dynamic pricing for stocked, nonperishable items is more difficult to rationalize, expect companies to begin experimenting in this area soon. While the ability to order more product does change the nature of the problem, this is the area where the greatest impact from this method of pricing may be felt.

Rewards and Consequences

As technology makes dynamic pricing a possibility and as early implementers of this method achieve significant competitive gains, the widespread adoption of dynamic pricing across a broad product range seems inevitable. The ability to change product price easily and systematically over time can create an advantage that is very difficult for competitors to overcome. This may lead to consumer advocacy as the realization dawns that followers forced into dynamic pricing may never be able to catch up to the industry leader. The algorithms required to operate effective dynamic pricing are highly complex and challenge the largest computers' capacity. As the algorithms are executed, they generate data that increase their future effectiveness. It takes a clever team to operate these systems effectively and, as experience builds up, larger problems can be addressed and improved solutions implemented. The follower may never be able to climb the learning curve fast enough to reach the same proficiency as the leader. The result will be a lessening of competition. But what of the upside?

Widespread dynamic pricing will catalyze some significant changes. The retailing world will be quite different when prices of all products can change every hour and management must decide how much to sell rather than what prices to set. How will the consumer react? The evidence so far is quite positive: consumers have adapted to and gained advantage from the dynamic pricing of services — full flights mean lower fares. While it may take some time for consumers to adjust to more widespread, flexible prices, the net result should be lower average prices as spoilage is reduced and inventories are better managed.

Dynamic pricing is a leading-edge example of how information can be married with human knowledge and sophisticated algorithms to produce a formidable competitive weapon. It is here now and is already changing the nature of markets.

Adapted and reprinted with permission from Ivey Business Quarterly

Defending Your Local Brand Against the Megabrands

Niraj Dawar

Niraj Dawar is a professor of marketing at the Richard Ivey School of Business.

As trade barriers disintegrate around the world, previously protected markets are experiencing a deluge of international brands made powerful by the backing of enormous resources, state-of-the-art technology and global marketing experience. Global players, seeking sales growth and respite from their intensely competitive and saturated home markets, are rushing into these emerging markets. The invasion of international megabrands is rapidly transforming the once-expansive global village into a shrinking marketplace. The results of this onslaught have often been devastating for local brands, long accustomed to protection. The less prescient brands have been caught unaware. Their unpreparedness has caused the erosion of their market share, which, in many cases, is paving the way to their eventual demise.

But many local brands are defending themselves from the invading global megabrands, adopting two complementary approaches to survival. In the first approach, they exploit their knowledge of their local market in order to surpass the transnationals — at least in their home market. And in the second approach, companies with local brands emulate the new competition and expand internationally in order to achieve the scale necessary for survival.

Exploiting Local Knowledge

Nowhere is the impact of fallen trade barriers more apparent than in Russia, where a barrage of foreign brands swept in as soon as the economy was liberalized. However, in some industries, liberalization has entered a new phase — local firms have begun to put up a fight. For example, local computer firms in Russia are making inroads against such stellar competitors as IBM, Compaq and Hewlett-Packard. Although these American giants retain a strong hold on some market sectors, such as government purchases, local computer firms are learning the trade fast. Not only have local firms cornered more than half of the domestic market, they are growing faster than their international rivals in the US$1.5 billion personal computer market. In 1997, the leading local computer manufacturer, VIST, sold PCs accounting for 20 percent of the total market — more than any single foreign brand. VIST's success lies in its ability to meet local market needs. Recently, as the market shifted from government purchases to private consumers, VIST and other local manufacturers captured a significant portion of the growth by spotting and reacting to the shift earlier than foreign competitors.

In addition, local firms are capitalizing on their ability to deliver localized products and services. VIST can offer consumers the guarantees and service — including manuals in Russian — they require. And by having the country's largest dealer and support network, VIST has created an entry barrier for most competitors. As a result, American imports that only four years ago sold at double the price of homegrown brands today sell for only about one-third more.

Local brands do have one big advantage over global ones: the market positioning of global brands is an open book. Consumers and marketers around the world know that Pepsi is positioned as "the drink of the next generation," and that Pert Plus shampoo (or Wash and Go or Rejoice, as it is known in other parts of the world) has a convenience positioning. Since a global brand's positioning is known before it enters a market, and because it is often bound by this position, local competitors can pre-empt it by launching line extensions or new brands.

In India — another large and newly liberalized market — the largest local distiller, United Breweries (UB), anticipated the entry of foreign competitors and launched several premium single and blended malt whiskies. As a result, they restricted foreign entrants to the small — although still profitable — super-premium market segment.

Local manufacturers in Brazil, Russia, Indonesia, India, China and other liberalizing markets sometimes take comfort in their cost advantage over international brands. Their products, designed and produced with local raw materials and inexpensive labor, offer a price advantage that foreign competitors cannot match. However, this advantage is often illusory. Local manufacturers often cannot duplicate the quality of international brands, and when they do, the cost advantage generally evaporates. In addition, international brands often adopt a long-term market entry strategy that allows them, over time, to take advantage of both the inexpensive local inputs and their superior technology. For example, detergent manufacturer Unilever produces using local raw materials and labor, while adapting its product quality to suit the local market — the Surf powder detergent made and sold in Indonesia is not the same as that available in South Africa. Yet Unilever's marketing is world-class in every market it is in.

If local firms can produce products of a quality similar to that of international players and still retain their price advantage, they should consider expanding into the international market.

Going International

Indonesian tobacco firm Hanjaya Mandala Sampoerna (HMS) exemplifies the need for a local company to go global in the face of stiff international competition. HMS derives 98 percent of its sales from the local Indonesian market. But, as large Western tobacco firms facing declining sales in their home markets have been driven to new stomping grounds in Asia, HMS's large local market has been increasingly under threat. Recently, HMS joined forces with another

Indonesian company, the Salim group (whose flagship company, Indofood, is the world's largest manufacturer of instant noodles), with a view to taking HMS's key product, the kretek (a clove cigarette), to international markets. Enormously successful in Indonesia, the kretek currently accounts for nearly 90 percent of tobacco sales — a success HMS believes can be replicated in other countries. HMS is establishing a presence in Malaysia, Myanmar, the Philippines and Vietnam, and plans are under way to market the kretek in Latin America. If HMS's international ambitions succeed, it will have a better chance of survival in the face of international competition than if its focus was only on protecting its domestic market position.

While several market entry strategies are available to firms intending to install themselves in overseas markets, establishing a brand ensures a profitable long-term presence. However, brand establishment is expensive and risky in the short term, and not all firms have the resources necessary to try it. But India's biggest luxury watchmaker, Titan, is attempting to do just this.

Titan's attempt at establishing an international brand is driven by its need to defend its domestic position. While imported watches are currently banned in India, this decades-old protection is expected to be phased out as a result of negotiations taking place at the World Trade Organization. Watch components are already being freely imported, and several international watchmakers, including Japanese conglomerates Seiko and Citizen, are set to take advantage of lower labor and capital costs by locating manufacturing and marketing operations in India the moment the trade barriers fall.

Titan's management admits that India's poor reputation for quality exports has traditionally been a hindrance to establishing a brand presence. So, when launching its watches in Europe in 1995, Titan's distinctive advertising campaign attempted to remedy this problem. Featuring the coy caption, "No one country could have made faces this beautiful," the advertisement is accompanied by the legend "French-Swiss-Indian-Japanese." This advertising strategy is more than a reference to the foreign collaborations involved; it is an attempt to make the product more "international" and appealing to European consumers by disguising its "Indianness." It appears to be succeeding — Titan now has a 2 to 3 percent market share in Europe, compared with the 10 to 15 percent market share held by each of its largest competitors.

Private Branding

While Titan is ambitious and tenacious, its route to brand-building has been fraught with difficulties, including a lack of resources and foreign currency. Fortunately, brand-building, while a profitable long-term approach, is not the only means of developing a presence in international markets — unique opportunities are appearing. For example, many retailers in developed markets have introduced their own brands, opening up markets for international manufacturers. These retailers' products are often sourced from a few suppliers who find the large sales volumes attractive — especially since they do not have to expend time and effort building brand awareness and consumer loyalty. With increasing control over consumers' buying decisions, retailers are realizing large market shares for their private-label products. And increasingly, they are sourcing these products internationally. Such contracts provide an unparalleled opportunity for manufacturers in newly liberalized markets to enter large, profitable markets where they can threaten the very branded-goods manufacturers that are making the competition in their home markets so intense.

The private-label approach offers two advantages that are necessary antecedents to being a global player: it provides economies of scale without the costs and risks associated with brand building; and, because private label contracts specify stringent quality requirements, local manufacturers are being forced to upgrade quality to international standards and rethink their processes. Competing on the shelf with more established brands also provides valuable experience that can be used back home.

The entry of large multinational brands into previously protected markets is certainly a threat to those local brands that are unprepared for such competition. However, as economies become more liberal, local firms must recognize the new competitive environment and respond to the new challenges. Firms that pine for the days of protected markets will likely miss the new opportunities. But those firms that understand the challenges and opportunities, and use them to their advantage, have the best chance of surviving — and even thriving.

Product Defects: Turning a Crisis into an Opportunity

Niraj Dawar

Niraj Dawar is a professor of marketing at the Richard Ivey School of Business.

Companies make significant investments in developing their company brand in the minds of consumers and, as brand equity is founded in customers' perceptions, this valuable asset is extremely fragile. Today's products are increasingly complex and must be produced under heightened safety regulations. Managers fear the impact of an instance when a product is found defective or even dangerous. Such product-harm crises can have irrecoverable effects on customers' loyalty and their perceptions of product quality — and the organization.

Brand equity — the knowledge created for a brand in consumers' minds — is a very valuable and delicate asset that can potentially be devastated by publicity surrounding instances of defective or dangerous products. For example, the revelation by an independent North Carolina lab in 1990 that Perrier mineral water contained unacceptable levels of benzene, a carcinogen, and the subsequent ambivalent corporate response, led to considerable loss of market share and consumer loyalty for Perrier. The discovery of a product defect in Intel's Pentium chip three years ago showed that despite Intel's reputation for quality products, its ambivalent and tardy response to the situation left many consumers confused and upset.

But product-harm crises need not always be regarded as a threat — they may also present an opportunity. Research suggests that a company's response to a crisis combined with a good corporate reputation can help maintain or enhance brand equity. Take for example, the Tylenol capsule-poisoning incident in the early 1980s. Tylenol emerged stronger from the incident thanks to its impeccable reputation and exemplary response to the crisis.

Public relations strategies suggest that in order to protect brand equity in a crisis, firms need to take immediate and unambiguous remedial action. Yet many firms that find themselves in these situations display responses that range anywhere from stonewalling to unconditional support for their brand. Unconditional support includes a recognition that a problem exists, an apology for the problem, restitution for any damage or harm caused and remedial action to ensure that the event will not recur. Supporting the brand requires a firm to demonstrate that it is willing to stand behind the brand — even if it is very expensive to do so. This may mean communicating with consumers or other affected stakeholders through paid media or taking remedial action, such as instituting a product recall, setting up information hot lines, and compensating aggrieved parties. Denial of responsibility, lack of communication or inaction sends the message that a company is not supporting its brand. Many in the public relations industry believe that it was such a stonewalling approach by Exxon during the Valdez oil spill crisis of 1989 that hurt the company's reputation considerably.

Customers should see no ambiguity in a firm's response. In a product-harm crisis, an ambiguous response suggests inconsistent levels of support by the firm for its brand, and leads customers to a variety of interpretations. For example, a firm may admit to problems with a product, but not recall the product because it considers such measures as too drastic or expensive. This inconsistency of action can be very harmful to brand equity.

Studying the Effects on Brand Equity

Using a fictitious soft drink, the study first led participants through a fabricated product crisis in another city and then a launch of the same product in the participant's city. Varying the firm's response to the crisis and its pre-crisis reputation, we measured what happens to brand equity.

Findings suggest that reputation may moderate the impact of firm response on brand equity. A prior, customer-friendly reputation helps to provide at least a "buffer" and potentially a springboard for brand equity in times of crisis. But a firm with an ambiguous reputation may at best be able to preserve its brand equity in a crisis by consistently supporting its brand.

Both a good reputation and a company's past behavior develop an impression in the customer's mind about the firm and its future behavior. A company's reputation for customer-friendliness, for example, may affect consumers' expectations about the replacement of defective products, and more generally, about responsible behavior in a product-harm crisis. By making substantial brand investments under the public scrutiny provided by a crisis, firms demonstrate their commitment to the brand, and as a result, set themselves apart from firms that would not make such investments for fear of not recouping them through additional sales once the crisis has passed. Further, firms that stand by their brand but fail to make the associated investments necessary to protect themselves during a product-harm crisis are indistinguishable from firms that have no desire to salvage their brand. Consistency is key.

Firms that work to create a strong reputation prior to the crisis are building up a type of "insurance" against the impact of a crisis. Reputations are built over protracted periods of time and can be very costly. However, a good company reputation can be an extremely valuable asset in times of crisis. When a crisis strikes, it is too late to build a reputation — and a firm with no reputation must then live with the consequences. Managers must consider whether the cost of building and maintaining a positive reputation will pay off in the long run. Indeed, a good reputation is of valuable benefit to a firm regardless of a crisis situation. Results also indicate that, if a company with a good reputation aggressively supports its brand during a crisis, it may actually be able to improve brand equity. It's not advisable, however, for a company with a reputable brand to intentionally spark a crisis that it knows it can resolve. The risks are too great.

Finally, a company should make every effort to communicate with its customers and publicize its response to a crisis. And it may be necessary to tailor communications to different customer constituencies. For example, existing customers may be looking for confirmation that the firm is behaving responsibly in handling the crisis, while potential customers are focusing on the risks associated with the product. A product-harm crisis generates heightened media and public attention, which can be used to advantage in delivering targeted messages for different customer groups. If a firm is perceived by the public as not responding to remedy the situation, the consequences to brand equity may be severe — and even insurmountable.

Mining for New Product Successes: Seven Proven Strategies for Launching New Products

Allan J. Magrath

Allan J. Magrath is director of corporate marketing at 3M Canada Company. He holds an MBA from the Richard Ivey School of Business and is the author of six books on marketing.

New products are a potential wellspring for corporate vitality. New products excite customers, and bolster distributor and retailer confidence. They grow sales and profits, create jobs and benefit employees, communities, suppliers and shareholders. For example, Chrysler Corporation turned itself around with new products. Intel Corporation created huge shareholder wealth with such new offerings as Pentium and

Pentium Plus. And new product creation works just as superbly for low-tech products and services as it does for high-tech ones, as evidenced by the outstanding new product offerings for old-line manufacturers such as Rubbermaid, Black & Decker, Coleman and Gillette.

But despite the success stories, mining for new products remains a dicey proposition. Many fail or fall well short of marketers' expectations. Some new offerings merely cannibalize existing sales volume rather than add new growth. Still others fall short of being successful globally, even if they are successful locally. This whole area of management decision-making is clouded in the risk brought about by increasing consumer fickleness and invasive competition.

Seven Key Strategies

So how does one pursue a new product strategy with the best chances for success? Here are seven key strategies and some successful examples.

1. Mining Customer Complaints

Paying attention to customer complaints about what's already on the market can yield great new product ideas. Five of the top new-selling products in North America were developed from this kind of feedback. Kimberly-Clark's three-ply Cold Care Tissues answered complaints about two-ply tissues tearing from "heavy cold" users. Gillette's Clear Stick deodorants helped satisfy consumers who were unhappy about the white residue left on skin or clothing from non-clear sticks. Lancôme's Rouge Idole developed a transfer-resistant line of lipsticks in response to chronic complaints about residue left on coffee mugs, cheeks and collars. Mirro/Wear-Ever's Airbake insulated cookie sheets were developed to reduce the occurrence of scorched cookies — the number one complaint of consumers about oven baking cookware. As a result, Mirro's global market share has skyrocketed. Black & Decker's DeWalt line of cordless power tools was introduced to an immediately favorable market response with its 18-volt power system (versus 12 volts on most of its rivals), so professionals or do-it-yourselfers can get more run time and the extra power often lacking in cordless tools. These ideas surfaced from customer dialogue about what they found most lacking in cordless tools.

2. Mining Observed Behavior with Existing Offerings

Often, powerful new product ideas can emerge by watching customers use current products. Observations and photographs of how personal computers were used in homes — typically in cramped spaces and on smaller desks than in business offices — led IBM to design its highly successful Aptiva S series personal computer with the "real world" of the cramped home office in mind. IBM made the CD-ROM, diskette drive and power switch easily accessible in a slim console that takes up minimal space on a crowded desk. When closed, the keyboard sits atop the console, and the monitor has built-in speakers saving even more precious surface space.

When 3M observed customers in focus groups wrapping gifts, it noticed they awkwardly used one hand to hold the wrapping, one for scissors and needed a third for the tape dispenser. Consumers were observed pre-cutting tape pieces and putting them along their hand and wrist to allow the gifts to be wrapped efficiently with two hands. Noting this, 3M launched Pop-Up Tape™, a patented dispenser that fits like a wristwatch around a wrist and dispenses pre-cut tape strips. Mining customer-use observations has resulted in a new global product for 3M with very large potential.

3. Mining Customer Aspirations Versus Needs

Traditionally, marketing has focused on consumer needs as the springboard for new product generation. But needs don't necessarily reveal latent hopes or secret aspirations — these require a deeper knowledge of consumer psychology. Perfect-fitting jeans are frequently more a hope than an expectation when shopping. Levi Strauss mined this deeper psychology when it created its Personal Pair software, which assists customers by designing the perfectly-fitting pair of blue jeans for their own unique body shape. The jeans are made at the factory and delivered within two weeks. The Mazda Miata was a huge global success because it represented the fulfillment of three convergent aspirations: unique design in a convertible sports car; high reliability and quality in auto operation; and an affordable price. These aspirations typically didn't merge in a vehicle before the Miata's debut. High design often accompanied high price, and sportiness meant poor reliability in terms of operation.

4. Mining Neglected or Overlooked Customer Segments

New product or service offerings that tap into neglected or overlooked market segments frequently succeed. Paul Iams decided to market premium pet food nationally to "fussy" pet owners back in 1982. By 1996, Iams' sales had soared from $16 million to $500 million. Fussy pet owners had been an overlooked segment by everyone in the industry, including industry leader Ralston Purina Company.

One of Canada's fastest-growing specialty insurers is Kingsway Financial Services Company of Mississauga, Ontario. Five years ago its sales were less than $20 million; today, sales exceed $141 million. Why such a fantastic growth rate? Kingsway offers car insurance to drivers dropped by other insurers or considered too risky to underwrite. Interestingly, Kingsway made more than $11 million in profit on its 1996 sales — despite these "too risky to insure" drivers.

Coleman, the U.S. pioneer of such camping gear as lanterns and stoves, is currently selling a new line of smoke detectors of special appeal to the elderly. The detectors feature a large, "broom button" alarm tester so the alarm can be shut off after being triggered by burning toast or a smoking candle. It turns out that being able to easily shut off an alarm is very important for nuisance-type alarms. And using a broom handle to do so is a terrific feature for the elderly who often have difficulty reaching the small deactivator controls. By mining a neglected niche with this new entry, Coleman has gained share at a startling rate of 40 percent. Lives have been saved in the process since many customers get so frustrated with the trouble of deactivation, they pull batteries out and forget to replace them — sometimes leading to a fire tragedy.

5. Mining the Extremes of Science or Art

New products whose functionality or styling owe their success to very new science or art often succeed by turning the radical into the commonplace. Novartis used pharmaceutical science to conquer fleas on pets by providing a once-a-month pill for dogs and cats during the flea season. This flea control method is radical compared with the usual plethora of shampoos, soaps, powders, collars and other potions used. Novartis' product has been enormously successful, gaining the bulk of market share over the more than 200 individual remedies on the market.

3M is harnessing new science with its Privacy Film for windows. Frosted windows clear at the flip of a light switch with this new film, which harnesses the alignment properties of electricity with liquid crystal droplets laminated between glass and polyester film.

While radical science helps boost the impact of new products, so too does radical art and design: Chrysler's new Sebring automobile, with a sculpted body, is selling tremendously well. Canon's successful Elph camera has a unique shape and stainless steel body, and Lexmark's, curved-shaped, gold-colored jet printer 2030 gives new elegance to what has been a sedate category of products. These high-art products are doing very well in their respective markets by using new shapes, surfaces, colors and materials.

6. Mining "Holes" in Competitor Product Lineups

Sometimes the search for uniqueness is greatly aided by looking over the competitive landscape for holes in your rivals' offerings. Black & Decker is a master at this, continually coming out with very different products in very established, crowded categories. Its research and development people ask themselves "What if" questions in adding distinctive capabilities to mature products such as, "What if flashlights could allow for two-handed repairs?" The results are the "Snakelite" twistable flashlight and a flexible hose-handle floodlight.

John Deere's new product, the Gator, is an inexpensive off-road utility vehicle useful for transporting nearly any kind of cargo over any kind of land surface. Nothing else like it exists among rivals' off-road entries. Without any close competitor and because of the versatility offered to so many markets, Deere dealers cannot keep this new product in stock. So successful has the vehicle been that Deere is extending the line of Gators to the golf course market. The vehicle's high-floatation tires allow equipment to be hauled around without risking damage to expensive and fragile greens.

7. Mining Lead-User Customers for Applications

Lead users in markets are those customers or companies with advanced foresight about new product possibilities. With a propensity to try new things and a forward-thinking lead position in its market, a firm can get a head start on new applications. 3M greatly boosted the success of two of its fastest-growing new products by piggybacking lead-user insights and adoption. Dual Brightness Enhancement film for laptop computer screens was adopted early by Toshiba, and 3M's line of microflex circuits grew rapidly from its association with Hewlett-Packard's printer division.

And this technique is not limited to launches of high-tech products. Eastman Kodak Company is pioneering digital camera successes with lead users in real estate and insurance adjusting where the digital conveyance of pictures is more important than image quality. Similarly, Shrade Company's Tough Tool, a multipurpose folding hand tool with 21 attachments tucked up inside the handles (such as knives, wire cutters, rulers, screwdrivers and pliers), owes much of its sales success to lead users in the mountain climbing, ranching, camping and hiking markets.

Increasing the Chances for Success

New products will always be risky just by virtue of their newness to the world. Giving birth to the new is almost always chaotic and difficult — and exciting. But mining for powerful new ideas with these seven strategy suggestions can help mitigate some of the risks and bolster the chances that the uniqueness of your idea emerges to the applause of end users in your chosen marketplace.

Adapted with permission from Ivey Business Quarterly.

Succeeding with Micromarketing

Michael R. Pearce

Michael R. Pearce is a professor of marketing at the Richard Ivey School of Business and co-holder of the Eaton NSERC/SSHRC Chair in Retailing. Kathryn Brohman, an Ivey Ph.D. candidate, assisted in the preparation of this article.

For retailers of products and services, new technology has delivered the ability to target large numbers of people individually. This has had a huge impact on retail marketing. Information technology has given retailers such a steady torrent of useful data about customers and product flows, they risk drowning in its flood if they don't learn how to take advantage of it.

This increased information flow is changing how decisions are made in organizations, and is requiring new competencies of marketers. While such skills as choosing product lines and dealing with customers remain critical for retailers, today's managers also need to be experts in data analysis and "micromarketing" — customized direct marketing techniques.

Information management has become critical to retail management. Increasingly, senior retail executives are being told they must invest in computers, software, data and competent people to stay competitive with the new ways of doing business. Yet there seem to be no ready guidelines about which micromarketing techniques are appropriate for which business purposes. There are no clear assurances that there will be adequate returns on these typically substantial investments and departures from current ways of doing business.

What is Retail Micromarketing?

Defining retail micromarketing is not difficult, but implementing it successfully is. For example, coupled with the increased use of the many time-tested methods of direct marketing such as catalogue retailing, are many new approaches such as database marketing, geodemographic-segmentation analysis, computer-assisted shelf management and interactive kiosks. All are considered aspects of retail micromarketing because they embrace both analytical techniques and marketing activities. A retailer cannot simply be regarded as being or not being a micromarketer, but rather must be considered in terms of degrees of involvement in micromarketing.

Mass Marketers vs. Micromarketers

Stripped to its essentials, marketing involves profitably managing one's relationship with customers. Mass retail marketers serve large numbers of customers in similar, if not identical, ways, targeting similarities across individuals and groups. In the extreme, global marketing refers to making basically the same offer to everyone. This offer can be, and typically is, adjusted to reflect some differences in large market groups such as cultural factors, leading to terms such as "multinational" and "regional" marketing. Mass marketers typically know little about their individual customers other than averages, such as average level of awareness or average transaction size. They often measure marketing productivity in terms of total returns on expenditures made, rather than in terms of impacts on small groups or individuals.

At the other end of this marketing spectrum is micromarketing, which includes, but is not limited to, one-on-one marketing. Here, an organization has a relationship with a very small group of customers, a household or family, or even an individual. Retail micromarketers think about a market in terms of customer-specific characteristics. Whereas mass marketing focuses on finding similarities across customers, finding the differences is central to micromarketing. Further, micromarketers believe that by customizing their approaches to customers, more lifetime profit can be obtained than by providing a standardized product or experience. Micromarketers "make a customer, not a sale" — they focus on the longer-term stream of revenues, not just the immediate transaction. Retail mass marketers differentiate products and services; retail micromarketers differentiate customers.

Driven by data, retail micromarketing gives organizations the capability to measure directly the value of their individual customers and the return on their micromarketing investments.

What's Involved in Retail Micromarketing?

To be successful, the retailer must engage in both microanalysis and customer-specific marketing — a complicated process requiring the micromarketer to profile, target, attract and retain customers.

COMPONENTS OF RETAIL MICROMARKETING

Profiling
- Geographic spotting then association
- Original data collection through point-of-sale research, customer research, etc.

Micromarketing Management
- Data-driven
- Performance-focused
- New competencies
- New obstacles

Retention
- Patronage incentive programs
- Post-purchase care programs

Targeting
- Customer worth valuation and ranking
- Database marketing
- Localized marketing

Attraction
- Tailored offering
- Addressed communications
- Unaddressed, but selectively delivered

1. Profiling

Retail micromarketers need far more information about prospects and customers than do mass marketers. Data about customer characteristics and responses to retail efforts are typically obtained in either or both of two principal ways. The first involves gathering individual or household data through a variety of methods, such as credit applications, survey research, clientele systems (where sales associates keep records of their customers' past purchases) and point-of-sale records. Critical to this process is the ability to identify individual customers or very small groups of like customers, ideally before, during and after purchase. The ability to track customers through these stages is possible through four activities:

- using customer identifiers, such as name or telephone number or assigned customer number;
- sensing or scanning devices that help relate that unique identifier to a database;
- database management that creates and updates customer information in a searchable form in a data warehouse (a large customer information system); and
- rigorous maintenance to ensure data are captured and used to keep the whole system accurate and current.

The second way involves the retailer's use of information collected by others to build a profile of a small group of prospects or customers. For example, when considering a new store location, a potential trading area around this site can be profiled using available government or commercial statistics. The retailer doesn't know the people here, but builds a detailed profile of them as a small group from these secondary data.

Alternatively, this kind of profiling can be done through "geographically spotting" a customer, then building a profile of that individual. Geographic spotting usually begins with learning the individual's home address, either precisely or approximately (such as with a postal code). This way of profile-building assumes that people who live in the same community have common interests, aspirations and buying patterns. If the retailer has access to commercial sources of information about the "neighborhood" characteristics (demographic and psychographic), then one might presume that the individual is like the neighborhood. The best-known commercial service that facilitates this kind of profiling in Canada is Compusearch.

Both profiling methods go beyond the typical customer descriptions done by many marketers. A mass marketer may know that an average customer buys a certain product 5.6 times in a year, but a good retail micromarketer will know exactly who bought what when — and often much more than this.

2. Targeting

Detailed profiling information offers the retailer many new ways of deciding which customers to seek out and how. Generally, target marketing refers to addressing oneself to some, as opposed to all, prospects and customers. Micromarketers learn what their individual customers are worth over time and thus can sort and target these customer segments based on their value to the organization.

3. Attracting

A retail micromarketer treats customers differently based on such factors as their unique characteristics or purchase histories. There are two basic types of attraction method: personal and impersonal. An example of a personalized method might be a letter addressed by name and mentioning specific personal matters, such as the last purchase made or an upcoming birthday. Such methods are common in direct marketing, but also include personal shopping agents, kiosks that reference a customer database record, or any other method of communication with the customer that is based upon personal information. The more information a retailer captures about a customer, the more powerful this approach becomes.

Impersonalized attraction methods involve unaddressed communications delivered selectively. In this instance the retailer does not have personal information, but does have some information with which to select prospects and customers from a mass market for a particular treatment. For example, a retailer may be intent on finding new customers with characteristics similar to those of current high-value customers. Based on knowledge of where these current customers live or what they particularly like, prospects may be selected to receive a particular promotional piece, a telephone call or something else the retailer has learned works well with current customers.

4. Retaining

Critical to successful retail micromarketing is retaining and developing valued customers, often called "loyalty" marketing. Micromarketers know that the cost of acquiring new customers usually exceeds the cost of retaining current customers — many know these numbers precisely. Using their intimate knowledge of what their customers are like and what they like to buy allows retailers to build on their relationship with individual customers over time. A good micromarketer tries to get a greater share of the customer's wallet by finding out what else can be sold to the customer, rather than looking for more customers to whom the same product can be sold.

Much attention has been paid to loyalty and retention programs — frequent buyer programs, continuity programs and frequency marketing. These programs share the characteristic of private "bonuses" (points or other currency the retailer offers to customers) exchanged for loyal behavior. In other words, these programs are "cold bonding" techniques — disguised discount programs that buy loyalty — and require excellent micromarketing skills to be successful.

A micromarketer looks for opportunities to customize based on recollecting individual differences. Many retailers have long known that "hot bonding" techniques that offer post-purchase personalized attention and care programs ensure customers feel valued and appreciated. These retailers are likely to provide follow-up satisfaction calls, prenotification of sales events and extra help with problems. For example, K. Barchetti, a U.S. fashion retailer, actually pre-alters clothes for valued clients before they arrive for a prearranged shopping visit.

Implications for Management

These retail micromarketing techniques have many implications for retail managers. The fragmenting customer market, increasing competition and the growing capabilities of information technology are all driving this phenomenon. However, retailers are finding they need to invest a great deal in new systems, in upgrading their employees' talents and skills, and in changing the way decisions are made. Retail micromarketing requires many changes in the way business is done, including new measures of performance, such as the lifetime value of a customer, share of customer purchases in a category and yield rates, and rethinking sales compensation practices.

Micromarketing also raises some interesting social issues, including a supposed reduced waste of resources due to more precise targeting. Proponents also claim that marketers are better at serving customers through more intimate knowledge of their needs and wants, their habits and attitudes. However, critics claim that marketers are invading personal privacy by collecting, using and selling for gain information about individual customers.

In one form or another, micromarketing is becoming mainstream in retailing, which means managers must not only learn about it, but understand which of these techniques is most effective, and under what circumstances. In fact, no choice between techniques is necessary — the key is to blend micromarketing with mass marketing to arrive at the most effective approach.

Expanding Your
Service Business

John Haywood-Farmer

John Haywood-Farmer is a professor of service management and operations at the Richard Ivey School of Business. He is exploring managerial problems in service quality, productivity and growth.

A restaurant owner was trying to decide how his restaurant should grow. Sid had some years' experience managing family dining restaurants and, after completing his academic studies, decided to get back into the industry and introduce TexMex food, his childhood favorite, to Canada. Eventually, his new restaurant in a suburban strip mall was up and running. After eight years, by all measures, it was a success. Customers were loyal and numerous, and the establishment was profitable. Even more importantly, the concept had stood the test of time.

Now Sid was thinking about where to go from here. He could open a second unit, possibly in the same metropolitan area. If it proved to be successful, he could later open more. He could also diversify his offering, perhaps by opening for breakfast or by broadening his menu. A third option was to buy an existing restaurant which he could then convert into his TexMex concept.

Most service companies, if they are successful, will reach a stage in their development where their next move — if they are to remain successful — requires deciding how their business should grow. Managers attempting growth for their service companies generally try one of three strategies: they expand the number of stores or offices they have (referred to as "multiplication"); they diversify the services they have to offer in hopes of expanding their market; or they acquire and convert other businesses. When deciding among these strategies, it is important to remember that each has its advantages — and its potential pitfalls. Knowing which strategy to select and which to avoid is no easy task. But careful analysis and planning can make growth not only possible, but highly profitable.

Adding More Stores

The most commonly used strategy to achieve growth involves geographically expanding the company-owned units or franchises an organization has. Most users of this strategy start with a single service site and spend the early stages of their company's development — possibly several years — refining their service concept. Eventually, they open a second site and soon more. Following such a strategy has resulted in some enormous organizations. For example, in 40 years, McDonald's has grown from one store to more than 23,000 restaurants worldwide today. Despite the fact that its North American restaurants are struggling, McDonald's is still expanding its number of stores worldwide.

Successful multiplication requires a sound, robust service concept that is focused — in that it is internally and externally consistent — and designed to meet the customer's needs. A good concept builds on the four P's of the traditional marketing mix — product, place, price and promotion — by adding participants, physical evidence and the service process to the mix.

Participants include both customers and staff who interact with them. Train your staff well, as there is often a high level of direct customer interaction with service personnel during service production and delivery.

Physical evidence is another necessary component, because many services are intangible. Thus, customers need physical cues to give them information about what the service is like. Finally, the process is important, because of customer involvement in service production; indeed, many managers believe that service itself is a process.

For a service organization to be internally focused, it must align each of these seven elements of the service concept — nothing should seem out of place. Sid's TexMex restaurant has an internally consistent concept. It emphasizes authenticity — recipes from the Texas-Mexico border area, mesquite charcoal, longhorn beef and "Texas-sized" drinks and steaks. It is licensed and offers table and bar service. Its tables, chairs and booths are simple with the decorations dominated by ranch and other regional artifacts. Its prices are moderate and its portions generous. Staff are friendly and dressed casually — jeans and western shirts are common. The facility is promoted in local news media. The process is standard for a full-service family restaurant; the location is on a major traffic artery, with easy access and ample parking.

To be externally focused, the organization should design its marketing concept to meet the identified needs of a specific target market. Sid's clientele are largely local people who come for a relaxing lunch or dinner. They are interested primarily in the food and the friendly atmosphere.

The best time to make a major adjustment to a service concept is when the organization is still small. Imagine the difficulty McDonald's would have if it had to apply a radical concept change — such as offering table service or alcoholic beverages in its stores — across 23,000 restaurants spread around the world. Concepts will change as an organization grows, but such changes will normally be evolutionary rather than revolutionary; they will occur in response to changes in the competitive environment, such as changes in customer tastes and competitive developments.

Growth through a multiplication strategy also requires a control system that lets senior managers manage at a distance. Because no person can physically be in two places at once, adding even a second business site will demand something more than line-of-sight control. The new scheme will include systems of accounts that allow the manager to take the organization's pulse at any time from printed or electronically displayed information. It will also include a means to evaluate staff.

To manage at a distance, managers need to know how to delegate and have the mental and emotional readiness to do so. They must be confident and trust their people and system. Of course, this assumes that they have staff who are competent enough that responsibility can be delegated to them, and that managers have enough people to do the work. It also assumes that sufficient financial resources are available to provide for fixed assets and working capital.

Growth through multiplication requires the addition of site selection and site development activities within the organization — or at least the ability to outsource them wisely.

Any growth by multiplication will inevitably lead to a portfolio of managers or franchisees, each with a different degree of experience and with needs that vary from those of head office. It is an ongoing challenge to design a system that recognizes these differences, is reasonably fair, is easy to administer and provides people with what they need.

Adding More Services

Rather than adding more sites, a service business can grow by adding to the services it offers. Such expansion through diversification of offerings usually occurs in organizations with high fixed costs and with a large fixed asset that has unused capacity. For example, many successful ski operations eventually try to become four-season resorts, offering hiking, golf and sailing in what had once been their off seasons. Sports stadiums that initially supported only baseball or football soon began catering to multiple markets, offering their facilities for such events as concerts and trade shows in addition to other sports.

The major challenge in growth through diversification is keeping the service concept intact, or at least changing it in a planned way. It is inherently difficult to design and staff facilities that simultaneously suit multiple activities or audiences. Consider baseball, ice hockey, football, track and field, tennis and basketball. A facility, such as Toronto's SkyDome, that is ideal for one might be quite unsuitable for the others. But economics often force stadium architects to build flexibility into their designs. Inevitably, the results are compromises that are acceptable to many, but ideal for none.

Diversification can lead to staffing conflicts. Staff who are suitable for one type of business or group of customers might be less than ideal for others. For example, a concert hall with staff skilled in catering to the tastes of a classical music audience might encounter problems if it uses the same staff as it attempts to diversify into the country and rock music markets. The potential for misunderstandings and reduced service quality is high.

Diversifying the services offered can attract a new customer group that is different in many ways from the original set of customers. Should each group want to do business with your organization at the same time, the presence of one group might reduce the service quality to the other. For example, groups of loud, boisterous snowboarders are bound to interfere with groups of younger children learning to ski on the same slope. Neither group will get the service they would like until they are separated, either physically or temporally. And, even if the groups do not conduct their business with you simultaneously, the image one group represents to the other might remain associated with your organization — with a possible result being the loss of one group as customers. Potential clients often judge consultants or accountants, for example, by finding out who their clients are.

Buying Up and Converting Other Businesses

A service business might grow by acquiring existing businesses that it then makes a part of its existing operations. Although this strategy can result in rapid growth, increased market share and the elimination of a competitor, problems can arise. Managers need to understand what they are really acquiring, which could be anything from an operating system to real estate to people and skills to a customer base or to a reduction in competition. It doesn't matter what is being acquired, as long as it is real and has sufficient value to the acquiring organization. Unfortunately, some purchasers get so caught up in the chase for growth through acquisition that they lose sight of the need to take a long, objective view of an acquisition's real value.

Some managers forget, or don't understand, how difficult it can be to merge different operating systems. Many mergers negotiated by senior financial and strategy executives seem to ignore the difficulties of merging operations. For example, equipment and software used by two different operations often don't fit together well. And many times, the various people from differing operations don't fit well either. Customers can be very unforgiving when problems arise as a result. However, involving operations people early in the merger process and investing in adequate training can reduce such problems.

Keep an Eye on the "Real" Business

Any growth has the potential to be exhilarating. But if handled poorly, growth can "sink a sailing ship." Many managers get so caught up in managing the growth itself that they lose sight of their organization's real business — making good products and services, and selling these to their customers. Losing customers through inattention to operating detail and to changes in customer needs can result in a dramatic reduction in cash flow just when the organization needs it most. The results can be sad for all involved — staff, managers, shareholders, suppliers and customers.

Sid has lots of opportunities, each with its potential pitfalls. He is carefully examining his options, and such care will help him to make the right decision. His financial strength and independence also allow him the luxury of being able to take his time and refuse potential opportunities. With his successful concept and the time to plan, Sid is in an enviable position.

IV
International Strategy:
Seizing the Opportunities

International Business: The New Ethics

David Sharp

David Sharp is a professor of managerial accounting and control at the Richard Ivey School of Business and has interests in international ethics.

The history of multinationals is liberally sprinkled with stories of questionable business practices — illegal payoffs and influence peddling among them. But a new consensus is emerging — the bad old days of international business are past, and business in the 21st century is to be conducted in an ethical and socially responsible way. That is not to say that operating an international business in an ethical manner is easy, but managers should not allow the challenges to discourage them from doing so. Today's manager now has a responsibility to operate not only profitably but to do so within ethical boundaries. According to Courtney Pratt, president of Noranda, in an address to the Canadian Club: "A company has a responsibility to a broader constituency than its shareholders . . . a company can meet its responsibility to create value for its shareholders only by seeing the world in this way."

Challenges of the Ethical Approach

What is ethical business behavior? A broad definition suggests that, in addition to meeting all applicable laws, ethical business behavior balances the rights of all stakeholders in an equitable and responsible manner.

What kinds of ethical problems do managers face in the international business arena? Some arise from cultural differences — that is, differences in norms of acceptable behavior in different parts of the world. Values differ across national borders — and even within them. For example, gender and age discrimination are not only acceptable practices in certain countries outside North America — in some areas they're legalized. Tom Donaldson, an American writer on multinational ethics, suggests that where a difference between local and home values exists, managers should apply whichever is the higher standard. In practice, this means, at the very least, meeting the expectations of all countries. In some cases, companies may choose to exceed situations where there is a lower standard in favor of maintaining their own value standards.

Probably the most challenging issue involves "questionable" payments. Many kinds of payments to various levels of government officials are highly suspect in Canada — and illegal, according to the United States' Foreign Corrupt Practices Act. Yet they are often standard practice in many parts of the world. Managers should be aware that the problem is like a "slippery slope" — once a company has paid even a small bribe, word spreads. Saying "no" is more difficult the next time it happens — and there will be a next time. Too often, unsuspecting expatriate managers are lured by self-serving officials into the belief that bribery is the only way business can be conducted. In the long run, it will be easier and less costly to say "no" up front, even if, in the short run, a company loses business. Although such practices may indeed be widespread, it does not mean that they have to be followed. Indeed, there are companies that do not do business in certain countries because their management holds a moral point of view and abides by it. For instance, in 1992, Levi Strauss decided not to expand into China because of human rights concerns, despite the attractive commercial opportunities there.

There is a risk that managers assume that their norms are right and others' are wrong. Successful international management requires cultural sensitivity — a recognition that there are alternative, but equally acceptable, ways of doing things. For Western cultures, fairness, justice and individual rights are at the core of ethical behavior. But in other cultures, loyalty and social obligations often dominate. For example, North Americans generally frown on nepotism, but in many countries in the Middle East and throughout Asia, managers have a strong sense of loyalty to their extended family, clan, or in-group (school or university classmates). As a result, hiring decisions in many parts of the world are often heavily influenced by factors other than merit. While this may appear to North Americans as unfair, it is nevertheless a widely accepted practice. It is no more unethical, from a loyalty perspective, than is hiring on merit, from a fairness perspective. There are even certain advantages to this approach — a greater sense of employee loyalty often exists, for example.

Consider, too, that there may be another way of interpreting the situation. For example, although offering questionable payments is a practice that is clearly unacceptable according to North American values, making "facilitating payments" is a widespread and entirely legitimate practice in some parts of the world. The manager must learn to distinguish between those practices that are acceptable, legitimate and normal according to the standards of the host country, and those that are not.

Another source of ethical problems is the abundance of opportunities for questionable decisions. There are choices to be made and conflicts to be resolved which simply have no one-country counterpart. Transfer pricing is one example: even in a domestic context, transfer pricing, or shifting profits between divisions, is a contentious issue. But in an international context, shifting profits from high-tax to low-tax countries, for example, can reduce a firm's overall taxes to the benefit of shareholders, but at the expense of the high-tax jurisdiction — often a developing country. Taxation authorities try to limit the extent to which transfer pricing manipulation is possible, but the reality is that most multinationals devote enormous resources to global tax minimization. Whether managers should take full advantage of transfer pricing flexibility, or even unintended loopholes in developing country legislation, raises questions of fairness to host country governments.

The inequity of power between multinationals and developing countries introduces other concerns. The economic resources of the largest multinationals exceed those of many small — and even mid-sized — nations. Managers can wield powerful political influence, and often have a better understanding of the economic consequences of legislation than the legislators themselves. Thus managers should execute their responsibilities in a manner that is both fair and equitable to their shareholders and the stakeholders in their host countries.

Guidelines for Ethical Behavior

How can multinationals ensure that their managers behave in a socially responsible way while balancing shareholders' interests with those of other stakeholders? The most useful approach is establishing a well-understood corporate code of conduct which spells out clearly the values to which the company subscribes. Johnson & Johnson's brief but lucid "Credo" is a good example of a code that sets out the beliefs to which its management adheres. Some companies require their managers to read and sign a statement that they have read their company's code, often on an annual basis.

A code can be much more than just a guideline for managerial behavior. It can provide direction and support to managers on the front line of the corporate ethics battlefront. By providing ethical guidelines, such as how to handle bribery payments, it provides a manager with an "out." When in a difficult negotiation position with a customer, supplier, or government official, for example, the manager can point out that he or she simply has no authority to make such a payment decision. The guidelines of a code should be broad enough to allow a manager the flexibility he or she needs to apply them to specific situations as they arise. A code that is too specific may generate a legalistic — and consequently self-defeating — culture in the firm. A code should also be culturally sensitive, allowing managers to respect different local cultural norms. One approach to developing a code involves reviewing the codes of other companies and tailoring them to your company's corporate values.

However, a code in and of itself is nothing unless it is backed by a corporate culture, values, and most importantly, reward systems that are consistent with it throughout the organization. Too often, managers in otherwise responsible organizations are put into positions of having to meet narrowly defined revenue or profit targets made unrealistic by inflation, devaluation, or other adverse macroeconomic conditions. A manager under pressure to meet short-run profit targets is understandably less likely to give consideration to the firm's integrity if it costs him or her a bonus. Even well-intentioned managers are sometimes forced to compromise both their personal and corporate values because they are essentially rewarded for doing so. Multinational management reward systems should have enough flexibility to recognize the consequences of the higher risks of international operations, and should reward beyond profit returns alone. How many managers are actually rewarded for walking away from a profitable deal because it involved a questionable payment?

For the front-line manager facing a request for a questionable payment, there are a number of steps that can be taken. First, find out if this type of payment is legal in the country. It may be if there is no attempt to hide it. Second, determine if the payment violates the spirit of the firm's code of conduct. If so, are there alternative solutions? Again, it's necessary to correctly interpret the situation. In some countries, what appear to be requests for bribes are simply requests for bonuses, such as traditional holiday gifts for a company's employees. A careful inquiry into the purpose of the payment may not only save embarrassment but may also introduce an alternative way of making the payment, such as purchasing the gifts together with the requester. However, if after taking these steps the request still appears suspicious, then it is time to get help — share the problem with a supervisor and get input from the internal audit and legal departments. If any concerns arise from these sources, you may have no choice but to walk away from the deal, no matter how adamant the person making the request may be.

Maintaining a firm's integrity can appear to be costly in terms of lost business, and there is no doubt that in the short run a firm will indeed lose business to competitors with looser ethical standards. In the long run, though, a good corporate reputation is a valuable asset and pays handsome dividends. Not only does an ethical climate within the firm lower the risk that the firm might find itself in a difficult legal and public relations situation, it makes the job of managing easier. Further, it can attract customers and prospective employees who know that they will be treated fairly. And that is an important competitive advantage.

"Business is a critical element of society. It inevitably has a great impact on how society develops. It has a responsibility to play that role with high ethical and moral standards — with consciousness and with purpose," adds Courtney Pratt. In the end, the final argument for good corporate citizenship is not only that good ethics means good business, but that corporate social responsibility plays a key role in building a better society.

Suggested Reading

•Cohen, J., L. Pant and D. Sharp. "Culture-Based Ethical Conflicts Confronting Multinational Accounting Firms." *Accounting Horizons*, September 1993.

•Dalla Costa, J. *The Ethical Imperative: Why Moral Leadership Is Good Business*. HarperCollins Publishers Ltd. 1998.

•Donaldson, T. *The Ethics of International Business*. Oxford University Press. 1989.

•Michalos, A. *A Pragmatic Approach to Business Ethics*. Sage Publications. 1995.

•Nielsen, R. "What Can Managers Do About Unethical Management?" *Journal of Business Ethics*, Vol. 6, 1987.

An Old Rival Teaches New Tricks

Andrew Delios

Andrew Delios is a graduate of Ivey's Ph.D. program. He is currently a professor in the Department of Management of Organizations at the Hong Kong University of Science and Technology.

An old rival has been quietly emerging as a dominant global competitor. Japan's business community, notorious for its strength in exporting, is developing equally strong foreign-based operations in many
sectors of the home economies of North America,
Europe, Asia and, most recently, China. And what
we've learned about Japanese companies' success in
foreign direct investments holds valuable insights for
others looking to succeed internationally: they have a
pronounced tendency to use joint ventures; there is a
high degree of integration between their investments;
and the more international a Japanese company's
operations, the better its performance.

After years of competing with highly visible
Japanese-based electronics and automotive companies

that quickly penetrated markets with their exports, North American–based companies recognize the challenge posed by Japanese companies that have now begun to invest more heavily in production and sales facilities in Canada and the United States. But investment in North America makes up an increasingly smaller proportion of Japanese companies' international operations. Their investments in Europe are equally prominent, while those in Asia are becoming the nucleus of Japan's global competitiveness.

Japanese companies have long been interested in expanding sales in the markets of developed countries. In the 1960s, while most of their foreign direct investments were made in North America and Europe, Asia began to attract an increasing share of Japanese investment. By 1970, almost 40 percent of all Japanese investment was situated in Asia — a share equal to that held in North America and Europe combined. By the end of 1996, such investment in Asia accounted for nearly half of all existing Japanese foreign-based subsidiaries.

Since its investment restrictions were liberalized in 1978, the People's Republic of China has slowly emerged as a popular site for foreign investors worldwide — and for Japanese investors in particular. The rate at which Japanese companies have expanded into China is spectacular. In the first 12 years after China's reforms began, Japanese investors directed only about 4 percent of all investments there. But, between 1993 and 1996, China's share shot to 33 percent. Twenty years ago, almost no Japanese subsidiaries existed in China. Today, they account for 11 percent of all Japanese subsidiaries.

The progression of China and other Asian countries to more substantial standings in Japanese companies' portfolios of foreign direct investments is occurring as Japan also achieves greater prominence worldwide as a foreign investor. Since the 1950s, U.S.-based companies have consistently been the most active in making foreign investments, followed by companies from European countries, particularly the United Kingdom, France and Germany. However, during the late 1980s, the Japanese yen became stronger and Japanese foreign investments correspondingly cost less. The threat of increased trade protectionism in the United States and in Europe — because of the impending formation of the European Union — stimulated Japanese investment into these regions. In the last half of the 1980s, Japan

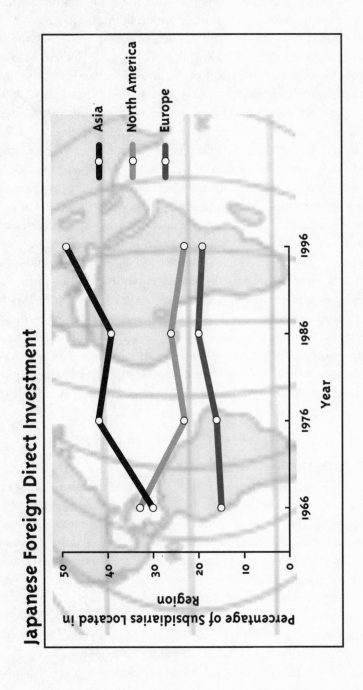

Japanese Foreign Direct Investment

Percentage of Subsidiaries Located in Region

Year

Asia
North America
Europe

averaged US$28 billion in foreign direct investments annually, establishing it as the leading foreign investor during this period.

The early 1990s saw the burst of Japan's "bubble economy," and it fell to fifth position. Yet in 1995 and 1996, as Japan's domestic economy showed signs of growth, foreign investment levels returned to match peak 1980s amounts, only to decline in late 1997 and early 1998, as the Asian Flu hit many countries in East and Southeast Asia, including Japan. Even with the late 1990s downturn in Japanese outward investment, Japan has maintained its position as a leading investor worldwide. As well, its position as the number one investor has solidified. Countries of Asia form the most important part of many Japanese companies' foreign investment portfolios, and when the effects of the Asian Flu subside, these countries will continue to be an important destination for Japanese overseas production and sales facilities.

Japan's success in establishing extensive foreign production and sales operations has three noteworthy characteristics. First, when investing abroad, Japanese companies are inclined to use joint ventures with other companies from the host country and with other Japanese companies. Second, their foreign subsidiaries' operations are often highly integrated as Japanese companies seek to transfer to international sites the very factors that made their domestic production efficient and competitive. And third, the more global its operations, the better a Japanese company performs.

The Japanese Preference for Joint Ventures

One of the greatest changes in mindset of international managers from the 1970s to the 1990s has been the recognition that alliances and joint ventures are fundamental to successful internationalization. Yet joint ventures continue to be plagued by the perception that they are overly difficult to manage and are transient organizational forms. But Japanese managers don't seem to share such perceptions.

The propensity to use joint ventures for international entries is greater among Japanese companies than with companies from other nations, especially those based in the United States. Among a sample of 18,000 Japanese foreign-based subsidiaries, 44 percent were joint ventures. The nearest comparable numbers for the foreign subsidiaries of U.S. companies places the U.S. propensity for joint ventures at 30 percent.

More important, this affinity for joint ventures is matched by their success in terms of longevity and financial performance. Of the almost 8,000 joint ventures we have tracked, 17 percent were established in the 1970s or earlier, with several having exceptionally long lives. For example, Brazilian auto parts manufacturer NHK Cimebra Industria de Molas Ltda. began in 1956 as a joint venture between Nippatsu — a Japanese company with 23 foreign subsidiaries — and Rassini 'auto parts' — the local partner. In 1995, this 51 percent Japanese-owned joint venture reported profitable operations on sales of US$32 million. Many other 1950s-vintage joint ventures continue to operate in such countries as Italy, Mexico, Taiwan, the United Kingdom and the United States, and in industries as diverse as manufacturing, trading and financial services.

For the 7,030 Japanese subsidiaries for which we have profitability information, those that are joint venture operations have the highest average performances, with wholly owned subsidiaries ranking second and acquisitions being the least profitable entry mode.

Integration between Foreign Subsidiaries

A unique aspect of Japanese business is the existence of *keiretsu* — groups of interconnected companies. Two basic forms of keiretsu exist. A horizontal keiretsu is an association of companies that operate in different lines of business; a vertical keiretsu is a group of companies stacked pyramid-like along a supply chain. A major listed company, such as Toyota, Toshiba or Hitachi, exists at the apex of these supplier networks, with several successively smaller companies forming the base. Keiretsu are often credited with providing several advantages to Japanese businesses. For example, vertical keiretsu allow for greater specialization within supplier firms, without inducing high transaction-related risks, thereby providing cost-based advantages.

Both horizontal and vertical keiretsu relationships are being replicated in Japanese companies' foreign investments. Among the best documented of these is the recreation of networks of suppliers by direct investment in the North American automotive industry. Equally conspicuous, but not as well known, is the foreign investment activity by smaller supplier firms and the extension of vertical keiretsu relationships to Japanese subsidiaries in Asia.

Among horizontal keiretsu, Japanese general-trading companies, such as Sumitomo Corp., Mitsui & Co., Mitsubishi Corp. and Itochu, are at the forefront of intersubsidiary integration. In terms of foreign assets, Japan's leading general-trading companies consistently rank among the top 50 multinational corporations. In 1996, Sumitomo Corp. and Mitsubishi Corp. owned more than 450 foreign subsidiaries, and Mitsui & Co. owned nearly 600. Many of these foreign investments are joint ventures with other companies from the same horizontal keiretsu. Mitsui & Co., for example, is involved in more than 70 investments in China, many of which are in textiles and involve joint ownership with Toray Industries, a Japanese manufacturer of synthetic fibers and a main member of the Mitsui keiretsu. Other subsidiaries have a more complicated ownership structure, involving several keiretsu partners. For example, Toray Industries, Mitsui & Co. and Mitsui Toatsu Chemicals Inc. each have a 17 percent equity share in Shanghai Mitsui Plastics Compounds Ltd., a US$9 million subsidiary located in Shanghai, China.

The More Global, the Better Japanese Financial Performance

Our research shows that Japanese manufacturing companies with more extensive international operations have higher profitability (return on assets, return on sales and return on equity). This trend exists irrespective of other influences on profitability, such as industry membership and the possession of valuable, proprietary resources.

Both the extent of exporting and foreign direct investment activities are connected to higher profitability. Export-intensive manufacturers, such as motor manufacturer Mabuchi Motor, sports equipment manufacturer Shimano, and popular games developer Nintendo — each of which derives at least 50 percent of its revenues from export sales — are among the most profitable of Japanese companies. Equally profitable, but more active in making foreign direct investments, are Canon Inc. and Fujitsu, as well as less well-recognized companies, such as electronic component manufacturers Omron Control and Mitsubishi Electric.

Companies playing on the global field must be aware of and able to respond to the challenges posed by the international operations of

Japanese companies. And nowhere is this more salient than in Asia, where Japanese subsidiaries proliferate and where the tight organization between subsidiaries may soon create challenges for other foreign entrants as great as those encountered when they try to enter Japan's domestic market.

Using Derivatives to Manage Risk

Steve Foerster and Dan Chiu

*Steve Foerster is a finance profes-
sor at the Richard Ivey School of
Business. He has consulted on
and written numerous case studies about risk management. Dan
Chiu is a graduate of Ivey's
MBA program.*

The past few years have witnessed an explosive
growth in derivatives usage among the world's
corporations. Most transactions have benefitted firms
tremendously, either in direct cost savings compared
to equivalent cash market transactions or in making
the corporate hedging process easier. However, the
international financial industry has been tarnished by
a few isolated incidents where derivatives were used
improperly. In preparation for another wave of possible derivatives problems, lessons should be learned
from some more notorious derivatives debacles.

Since 1994, derivatives have fallen under the
media spotlight. Recall the Metallgesellschaft AG
crude oil futures fiasco, rampant interest rate specu-
lators, Gibson Greetings and Procter & Gamble, and

the multibillion-dollar collapses of Orange County (due to over-leverage) and Barings Bank (due to a lack of internal controls while trading Japanese stock market futures). Throughout all this, the public has been peppered with smaller problems of derivatives gone awry, with Dell Computer Corporation, Air Products & Chemicals and a host of funds, including municipal, state pension and education endowment funds, falling prey. These problems generally didn't surface until a company's financial strain got so enormous that a press release was required to warn investors and stakeholders that the company was in serious difficulty.

Poor handling of derivatives has caused disasters in many unpredictable areas, including interest rates, foreign exchange and stock markets, and crude oil. It is unwise to be vigilant in one area just because disaster has recently struck there, and be complacent in another area because disaster has yet to occur.

Derivatives activity centers on financial risk management. All businesses face financial risk arising from changes in such market variables as commodity prices, interest rates and foreign exchange rates. For years, companies have used swaps, options and futures to adjust their risk profile so that it best suits their appetite for risk.

In debacles that have resulted in large losses, many believe that the risk management problems were caused by the company's lack of knowledge or expertise in derivatives usage. Many lawsuits filed by firms that have lost large amounts of money are based on the argument that they were duped into purchasing exotic derivatives. While a lack of knowledge or expertise may have caused some problems, little attention has been paid to the psychological side of managing a derivatives program.

In many instances where derivatives have been misused, egos overtook rationality. Rather than using derivatives objectively, users became addicted to a transaction's profit aspect. Instead of attributing the transaction's performance to market conditions, they believed they had developed an innate skill to outperform the market consistently. Simple derivatives evolve into complex, highly leveraged, highly illiquid instruments. And the moment fortune turns, panic often ensues.

Situations where derivatives usage evolved from straight financial risk-hedging vehicles to profit-generating trading vehicles have surfaced with corporate end users, mutual funds, college endowment funds, financial institutions and government investment funds. In some of the worst financial losses, the overseers of the derivatives program, such as the board of directors or the investment fund trustees, praised outstanding financial performance caused by derivatives gains. Rather than applaud the windfall, they should have recognized that sudden or large profits should be causes for alarm, not celebration. Such profits almost always result from large risks with equivalent or worse downsides. A good derivatives program helps a company reduce its risks, not increase them.

In today's leaner corporate structures, many treasury departments feel compelled to prove that, besides administering the company's finances, they add monetary value to the firm. More aggressive companies operate their corporate treasuries as profit centers. But this requires the same resources as a trading operation of a bank, including internal controls, systems and expert staff. Even with these resources, the merits of such an operation from the shareholders' perspective should be questioned. Shareholders wanting such an earnings stream could diversify their portfolio themselves. If a company treasury does not operate as a profit center, then management should question any derivatives transactions where the derivatives instrument's profile bears no resemblance to any of the company's risk.

The Risk Management Framework

The key to successful derivatives use is to have a well-thought-out process. To that end, the following three-phase framework presents the areas vital to all risk management programs — derivatives programs in particular.

Phase I: Identifying Risk and Determining the Desired Risk Profile

Quantify and qualify how much risk your company is willing to tolerate. For example, will it tolerate any fluctuations to its profitability due to foreign exchange swings? Is a seemingly insignificant fluctuation serious enough to warrant your attention? To answer such questions, follow three steps.

Risk Management Framework

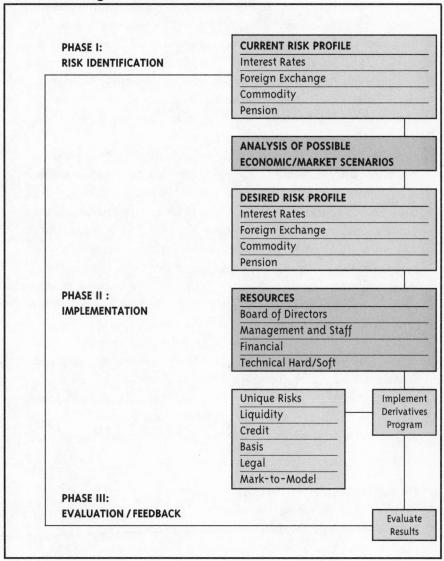

First, identify the market forces that may cause fluctuations to your company's profitability or asset values. Arrange corporate assets and liabilities, including those that are off-balance-sheet, into segregated pools whose market prices are subject to fluctuations due to a variety of market factors and conditions. Typical risk pools include foreign exchange risk, interest rate risk, commodity risk and pension risk. Separating corporate assets and liabilities into these pools allows an offset-matching process to occur. For example, foreign exchange risk in corporate assets is typically offset by an equivalent amount of foreign debt, eliminating the need to use derivatives to hedge foreign exchange risk. However, decide about those pools that have a net-risk exposure.

Second, consider just how much of the fluctuation, both favorable and unfavorable, is tolerable. Develop both realistic and less probable market scenarios under which the value of your company's financial assets and liabilities could change if no risk management takes place. For example, a company's pension assets could be dramatically affected by adverse fluctuations in financial markets. Although most companies leave pension asset management decisions to their investment advisors, they should quantify the cash flow and corporate pension expense implications of a large or prolonged downturn in the financial markets.

Last, set a target-risk profile based on economic and financial market outlooks, your firm's available resources and its risk tolerance. In your desired risk profile, you may almost eliminate risk or accept a particular risk level. For example, a high risk tolerance may mean that your company does not hedge completely its exposure to foreign exchange fluctuations.

Phase II: Implementation

In the next — and most important — phase of the framework, your company's desired risk profile is realized by coordinating resources and executing transactions necessary to achieve the expected results.

First, it is important to organize the necessary resources. An absence or failure of even one of the following resources is a sure recipe for disaster.

- *The board of directors.* Directors have overall responsibility in risk management. The board must consider and approve written risk management policies, including: its tolerance for risk and its general risk management philosophy; the scope of permitted treasury activity; guidelines for acceptable levels of credit and market risk; the structure and independence of the risk management processes and related organizational checks and balances; and accountability, at each appropriate organizational level, for the results of treasury activities.

- *Management and staff.* The psychological makeup of derivatives traders is as important as their technical knowledge of corporate finance, derivatives products and risk-management principles, and their financial market savvy. Several high-profile cases of derivatives problems involved staff who had an addiction to trading. Even programs with mandates to hedge risk only — with little flexibility — require those who execute derivatives transactions to make judgments regarding timing, magnitude of transactions and product specification.

  Obviously, a good corporate treasurer's profile is markedly different from that of a good trader. However, as treasurers also eventually function as traders to some extent, it makes sense that they possess some key traits of successful traders.

  Many other people within the corporation will be involved in the program, including those in accounting and internal audit. It is vital that they receive independent advice on their roles in the risk management process.

- *Financial resources.* The depth of a company's financial resources ultimately dictates the sophistication of its risk management program. Those with more financial resources can afford to have a higher risk appetite and correspondingly more sophisticated — and more costly — risk management systems. Typical costs for receiving up-to-the-minute financial market information via computer (for example, Reuters or Bloomberg terminals) are upwards of $20,000 per year per terminal. Software for managing financial risk and derivatives positions can cost more than $100,000 for more sophisticated systems.

- *Technological resources.* How sophisticated the technological resources need to be depends on the nature of the desired risk profile and the program's complexity. Typical systems provide market information, track risks, enhance the company's accounting systems and generate management reports, such as credit risk and market risk reports. Because of the highly specialized nature of today's risk management systems, external expertise is frequently a necessity.

Once the resources are in place, the derivatives program can be executed. A large corporation — with more than basic derivatives needs — will set up business relationships with several derivatives dealers, requiring many documents. The board of directors likely will have to pass a resolution authorizing the use of derivatives, the derivative program's scope, who will be making the transactions and who has signing authority. Then the company will have to negotiate an International Swap Dealers Association (ISDA) agreement with each of its derivatives dealers along with credit lines to facilitate transactions. If options are to be used, some dealers require that an options trading agreement be signed.

In addition to the legal requirements, companies also have to consider setting up a derivatives trading program that meets internal audit requirements. This mainly focuses on the separation of duties (for example, who initiates transactions versus who confirms them) and independent verification. External expertise is essential in setting up and monitoring a non-biased process.

Derivatives are usually more complicated than traditional cash instruments, such as foreign exchange, bonds or stocks, and require more than basic analysis. Of the risks (liquidity, credit, basis, legal and mark-to-model) examined, the two that most corporations should focus on are basis and mark-to-model risk. With basis risk, derivatives instruments are usually unable to replicate fully the risk of the underlying instruments. Consider a company hedging its interest rate exposure by entering into an interest rate swap. The interest rate swap may protect the company from a general rise in interest rates, but it will not help in the case where the company's credit rating deteriorates, causing the company to pay higher interest rates on top of a general rise in interest rates.

With mark-to-model risk, most companies may have simple computer models that estimate a derivative's price. A simple, low-cost spreadsheet may be all that is needed if your company does not complete many transactions or if the transactions are small. However, your company and its internal auditors should recognize that any model is only an estimate. You should also consider that the price generated by the model, even if accurate, is not necessarily executable. Liquidity factors play a key role for this aspect of mark-to-model risk.

Phase III: Evaluation and Feedback

Since your objective is to achieve a certain risk profile, you should ensure that this objective has been met. Was the risk profile appropriate? Were the assumed economic and market scenarios appropriate? How can the process be improved? The evaluation process should raise key questions about the risk management process that can be used during the next iteration.

To help in this process, you will need reports identifying market risk, credit risk and transaction limits. It is vital that companies canvass industry participants, industry peers and external consultants to come up with an evaluation process and reports that best meet their needs.

Planning Is Vital

If one overriding theme arises, it is that planning is vital. Establishing contingency plans to handle the most unlikely market scenarios and then swiftly carrying out those plans should be ingrained in all risk managers. In a moment of crisis, nothing is easier than putting into action a plan that has already been previously considered.

While analyzing a risk management program with some sort of framework may help to improve the program by asking the right questions, any risk management process is only as good as the people managing it.

Components of Current Risk Profile

- Foreign exchange risk arises primarily from either cash flow timing mismatch or balance sheet mismatch. Cash flow mismatches occur when, for example, revenues are in Canadian dollars while the cost of goods sold is in U.S. dollars to be paid at a later date. Balance sheet mismatches occur when a portion of the assets is in U.S. dollars. If there are no offsetting U.S. dollar liabilities, the corporation would incur a loss if the Canadian dollar appreciated, since the U.S. assets would be less valuable.
- Interest rate risk centers on the traditionally held belief that a debt's modified duration should equal the modified duration of the assets supported by that debt. In practice, most companies manage their debt maturity with a much more practical purpose. In a declining interest rate environment, companies usually keep maturities shorter, while in a rising interest rate environment they prefer longer-term fixed rate debt.
- Commodity risk ensues when a firm relies on a particular commodity, such as crude oil, newsprint or an agricultural product as an input for the product or service it ultimately provides.
- Pension risk arises when a firm has pension assets that are not sufficient to meet projected pension benefit payments.

Unique Risks of Desired Risk Profile

- *Basis risk.* The derivative does not completely hedge the underlying risk. This usually occurs in situations where an appropriate hedge instrument is unavailable and the company has to use a related instrument. For instance, there is no way of hedging the price of decaffeinated coffee, but a company can use coffee futures as an approximate hedge. The possible difference in price movement between the two commodities is the basis risk.
- *Credit risk.* A borrower will be unable to make timely interest or principal payments, also known as "counter-party" or "default" risk. This risk is quantified by setting aside a percentage of the notional principal related to the derivative, with the percentage dependent on the product's volatility.
- *Legal risk.* The person or company completing the derivatives transaction has no legal authority to do so, thus possibly nullifying the transaction.
- *Liquidity risk.* The derivatives holder will take a substantial discount to the current market price of the derivative in selling it. It varies with the size of the position relative to the market's size and the instrument's complexity. It can also vary with extreme market conditions. Holders of stock index futures contracts faced substantial liquidity risk when they tried to sell their futures contracts during the stock market crash in October 1987.
- *Mark-to-model risk.* The price generated by the derivatives holder's computer model and systems is not accurate. This is particularly important for companies using simple models to estimate the value of their derivatives holdings.

Adapted with permission from Ivey Business Quarterly.

Developing an International Technology Strategy

Tony Frost

Tony Frost is a professor of international strategy at the Richard Ivey School of Business.

The rapid expansion of the global economy over the past two decades has produced both opportunities and challenges for technology-based companies. On the one hand, the growth of overseas markets has meant that product development costs can be spread across a larger number of customers, increasing the returns while decreasing the risks of research and development. On the other hand, globalization has also meant that competition in those markets has intensified. In many industries, firms are struggling to compete with traditional industry rivals and also with competitors within those new markets who are becoming more technologically advanced and who may have built-in cultural and political advantages.

Over the last several years, I have been engaged in an ongoing research project with colleagues at the

Massachusetts Institute of Technology (MIT) that has looked at how firms are responding to these and other technology management challenges posed by globalization. Our research suggests that firms are responding in different ways and, not surprisingly, are experiencing different results.

Key drivers of the decision to internationalize R&D

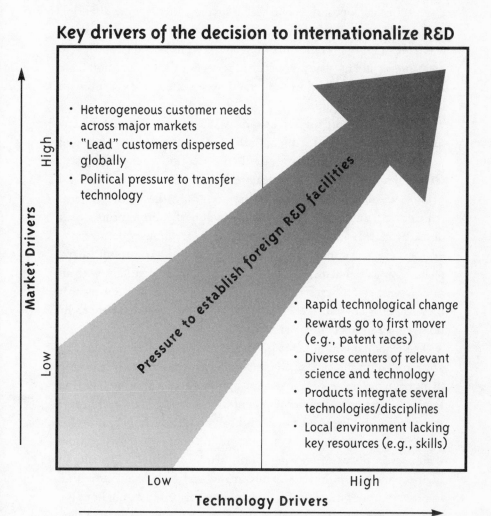

- Heterogeneous customer needs across major markets
- "Lead" customers dispersed globally
- Political pressure to transfer technology

Pressure to establish foreign R&D facilities

- Rapid technological change
- Rewards go to first mover (e.g., patent races)
- Diverse centers of relevant science and technology
- Products integrate several technologies/disciplines
- Local environment lacking key resources (e.g., skills)

Market Drivers (High / Low)

Technology Drivers (Low / High)

For managers in technology-intensive businesses, globalization poses two fundamental questions. This first relates to demand conditions — the "market pull" side of the technology management process: do firms have the technical resources and capabilities where they need to be in order to capitalize on the new market opportunities offered by the global economy? For many firms the answer is no. Traditionally, R&D has been the last function to internationalize. Most firms continue to perform the majority of their core product and technology development activities at home. For Canadian firms, who have historically been oriented toward the enormous U.S. market, this was, and in some cases still is, an appropriate and viable strategy. But as more attention shifts to the large and rapidly growing markets of Asia, Latin America, and Eastern Europe, companies from advanced industrial countries are increasingly finding that products and services developed at home are not meeting the needs of overseas consumers as effectively as firms with local technical capabilities.

Perhaps even more importantly, firms seeking to enter such potentially lucrative markets as China, Brazil, India and Indonesia often find themselves facing intense pressure by host country governments to transfer technology — often leading-edge technology — to local firms as a condition of market entry. Typically, these governments demand that multinationals establish technical joint ventures with domestic partners. The goals and processes of technology transfer may even be explicit conditions of these agreements. As a result, many technology-based firms find themselves, perhaps unwittingly, with an international R&D presence, and the daunting task of ensuring that these facilities are staffed and managed effectively, and that core technologies are protected.

The second question raised by globalization concerns the supply or "technology push" side of the technology management process: do firms have the resources in place to monitor and access the new and important technological developments that are affecting the industry? Again, for many firms the answer is likely to be no. Globalization has meant that countries — and regions within countries — matter more than ever in terms of creating world-class companies, especially in high-technology industries. Thus, many high-tech firms now find important centers of science and technology dispersed throughout the world, often in regional pockets or "clusters" such as Silicon Valley (computers and electronics), Milan (fashion and design), and Wall Street (finance). Moreover, research suggests that the knowledge originating in these regions does not travel seamlessly across borders, but remains embedded in the interpersonal and interorganizational relationships that characterize these centers. The challenge is to ensure that the firm is not blindsided by any important innovations occurring outside its field of vision.

One of the key lessons from our research suggests that best practice is contingent — there is no one right answer to the question of whether a firm should build an overseas technological capability or keep R&D concentrated at home. Industry conditions, the bargaining power of foreign governments and the capacity of the firm to coordinate and control a distributed network of R&D facilities all play a role in such a decision. What is clear, however, is that all firms need to develop an internationally oriented technology strategy, one that explicitly incorporates an international dimension into the technology management process.

A useful starting point is for senior managers of the firm to understand the key market and technology drivers in their industry that are bringing pressures to bear on the R&D function to go global. Market drivers are those forces that provide incentives to companies to customize products and services for local market conditions. Pressures placed on foreign firms by host-country governments to establish local R&D facilities for technology transfer are also considered market drivers. Where customer needs are heterogeneous across countries or regions, this will create pulls to locate R&D nearby. In some cases, local technical service (training, installation, support) or minor product adaptation may be all that is needed. However, in locations where market potential is especially large, or where customers have needs that place them at the forefront of market needs worldwide, firms may need to consider establishing product and/or technology development centers abroad. 3M, for example, serves the needs of the European leather industry from a product development facility in Belgium. The Canadian automotive parts manufacturer Magna International has an important R&D presence in Detroit, close to its major customers' product development centers. Indeed, with the increasing need for joint development in the automotive industry, the Detroit area has become a magnet for foreign and domestic suppliers. Similarly, Nortel uses its technical facility in Richardson, Texas — a main center of telecommunications R&D activity — to work closely with nearby customers such as MCI and Sprint.

There are also many technological factors that influence the costs and benefits of an international R&D presence. In industries where technology is changing very rapidly and where being a technological first mover is a key success factor (biotechnology, for example) firms face considerable pressure to locate R&D facilities close to centers of the most advanced scientific work. In recent years, many European and Japanese chemical/pharmaceutical companies have established biotech research facilities in U.S. locations such as San Francisco, Boston and New Haven, in order to participate directly in the local technological milieu. Many of these locations are associated with outstanding research universities such as Stanford, Harvard, MIT, and Yale.

Other relevant technology drivers include the diversity of the industry's technology base and the importance of scale. A recent trend in many industries — in part driven by globalization — is the creation of new products out of the fusion of previously distinct technical areas. Consider, for example, how digital technology is changing photography, or, more broadly, of the convergence of computers and communications. A manager from a major European automobile manufacturer recently discussed with me the concern his company has about the growing importance of microelectronics to the automotive industry. How, he asked, can his company, from its home base in Europe, possibly keep up to date with all of the new and diverse electronics technologies affecting the industry, many of which are being driven by developments in the United States? The answer is, it likely can't. The firm is currently considering several U.S. locations for establishing an advanced technologies research group.

Historically, the greatest force for maintaining a centralized home-based R&D organization has been scale or "critical mass," both in terms of people and equipment. Interestingly, our research suggests that scale economies may not be the barrier they once were to more geographically distributed R&D structures. We have seen many companies that have established small, focused, "niche" technical facilities in overseas locations. With limited mandates and tight linkages back to central R&D, these units can play an important role in the firm's technology strategy, for example, by developing specific components for a larger system or product, or by seeking out new, high-potential technologies for licensing or acquisition.

Understanding the major market and technology drivers is a key first step in formulating an international technology strategy. But it is only a first step. Many other considerations need to be taken into account, especially the firm's business strategy, its resources, and the capacity of its managers to deal with the organizational complexity associated with an international network of R&D facilities.

A New Generation of Global Leaders is Needed

Allen Morrison

Allen Morrison is a professor of multinational business management at the Richard Ivey School of Business and a graduate of Ivey's MBA program.

Finding effective global leaders is one of the greatest challenges companies face in today's international business environment. In a recent survey of more than 100 Fortune 500 companies, having competent global managers was cited as the factor most critical to achieving international success, surpassing such factors as financial resources, communications technology, quality local workforces, government assistance and freer trade. However, a sizeable gap exists between global market opportunities and the availability of leaders who can both recognize these opportunities and effectively implement global strategies. Closing the gap requires a significant change in mindset about what makes a good leader.

Western management theory is based on a strong belief in hierarchical command-and-control systems, thorough competitive analysis and strategic audits, and short-term profit objectives. In Canada, individuals who embrace these values become candidates for senior leadership positions. This is not dissimilar to what is happening in the United States. Americans love leaders like Jack Welch, Andy Grove and Lou Gerstner because their behaviors are consistent with the U.S. model of good leadership: they are decisive, aggressive, ambitious, intolerant of poor performers and have strong analytical skills. In Japan, where teamwork, market-share objectives and a commitment to quality are important, the saying "The nail that stands up gets pounded back down," describes the prevailing management philosophy.

Each country's beliefs are generated by domestic education and political systems, the media and powerful internal and external reward systems. Generally, people move into leadership positions when they demonstrate the competencies embraced by their national culture.

But the importance of relationships, short-term profits, hierarchies, ethics and risk-aversion are among a range of factors that vary between cultures. As the tidal wave of globalization sweeps the planet, practitioners and theorists have been forced to rethink age-old, culture-specific management models that don't stand up to what is required for a company to become a global player. For successful globalization, companies with global ambitions need leaders who can look beyond their familiar home-country approaches. What is required is a global model that can be applied everywhere. Such a model would transcend national schemes and be a powerful tool in recruiting, developing and retaining future leaders.

To develop this model, we set out to determine what competencies managers need in order to lead a company that has operations spanning a world of diverse cultures, capabilities and customers. Interviewing 125 top global leaders in more than 50 international corporations based in Europe, North America and Asia, we learned that for global leadership to be possible, global business savvy and global organizational savvy are both required.

Global Business Savvy

Leaders with global business savvy recognize global market opportunities for their company. According to Homi Patel, vice-president and general manager of manufacturing at General Motors Powertrain, "A global leader has a vision of doing business worldwide with the ultimate goal of making money." In other words, a global leader has global business savvy. He or she views the world — not just his or her home country — as the arena for value creation, a borderless marketplace in which "the sun never sets." Savvy global leaders continually emphasize the importance of international market opportunities when meeting employees. Virtually every staff speech made by General Electric's Jack Welch, Eastman Kodak's George Fisher, Sony's Nobuyuki Idei, the LG Group's Bon Moo Koo and Nokia's Jorma Ollila, emphasizes the crucial importance of global markets.

Leaders with global business savvy recognize three types of international market opportunities for their companies. First, they notice arbitrage opportunities, which involve cost and quality differences in production inputs. They scour the world for the cheapest and highest-quality inputs. They understand that the cost differentials for land, energy, labor and raw materials differ widely among countries. They know, for example, that although recent studies by the German Institut der Deutschen Wirtschaft and Statistics Canada show that the hourly rate for industrial labor in 1996 averaged US$31.76 in Western Germany, US$20.26 in France, US$17.50 in the United States, US$14.63 in the United Kingdom, and US$13.60 in Canada, they must balance these cost differentials with labor productivity measures. They know that real cost differences exist and can be exploited. For example, American Airlines processes all of its U.S. tickets in low-cost Barbados, and an increasing number of Canadian software companies subcontract work to low-cost Indian companies such as Tata Software.

Second, global leaders recognize the rapidly globalizing opportunities for their companies' goods and services. More than 70 percent of the world's markets exist outside Canada and the United States. Countries such as China, Chile, Ireland and Peru have seen their economies grow more than 8 percent annually during much of the 1990s. Not surprisingly, leaders such as Hisashi Kaneko at NEC, John Pepper at Procter & Gamble and Jean Monty at Northern Telecom have relentlessly expanded their companies into such new geographic markets in order to build revenues.

And third, global leaders look for efficiency gains that can be attained by eliminating redundancies, using company size as an advantage and capturing economies of scale. The ability to shave costs by cutting redundancies has been a major driving force behind Jack Smith's international expansion efforts. As General Motors' CEO, Mr. Smith has launched a US$2.2 billion program that includes building nearly identical auto assembly plants in Argentina, Poland, China and Thailand. GM's process technology is being standardized so that robots, software and computer systems are identical across all four plants, eliminating costly duplications in system design and engineering.

By eliminating redundancies, global leaders are also better able to exploit company size. For example, they can consolidate purchases and negotiate lower prices with vendors. They move beyond simply finding the cheapest inputs from around the world to effectively pressuring vendors to offer volume discounts. Depending on the input, IBM estimates that global sourcing has cut its component costs by between 10 and 35 percent.

Global leaders maximize efficiencies by reaping the benefits of economies of scale and of learning. Often, increasing production volumes moves companies quickly through the learning curve. For example, Airbus' first A300 aircraft took an estimated 340,000 person-hours to produce, while its 87th plane took just 78,000 person-hours. And maximum economies of scale are typically reached when volumes exceed the potential demand of virtually every national market. By standardizing output and selling to multiple markets, global leaders drive costs to their lowest possible levels.

To recognize global market opportunities, leaders need a broad and deep knowledge base. Savvy global leaders master fundamental international business principles, including those covering finance, accounting, marketing, human resource management, operations, relations, economics, industry conditions and strategy.

Global Organizational Savvy

Beyond a mastery of international markets, global leaders need an intimate knowledge of their own company. This global organizational savvy is required to mobilize their company's resources to capture global markets.

However, understanding and working with complex global organizations requires competencies that many managers lack. To the detriment of developing a sound understanding of the fundamental strengths and weaknesses of their company's more distant operations, some managers spend an inordinate amount of time familiarizing themselves with company policies and programs. They understand company rules, but not where critical knowledge and capabilities can be found within the organization. Many decision-makers know much about the global organization in an abstract sense, but lack a detailed knowledge of what is really happening in key markets.

Lack of organizational knowledge is an even bigger problem for managers posted outside their organization's head office. Often, they have only a limited sense of what the entire organization is about. Not surprisingly, their effectiveness in anything but the most local tasks is severely limited. Even expatriates who have lots of head office experience risk getting cut out of the information loop once they take an overseas assignment. One U.S. country manager for a Fortune 50 company in Asia complained that, although he had been away from head office for only two years, he felt lost about what was going on there. The people who sponsored his overseas assignment either had been reassigned to other jobs or had largely forgotten their promises to keep him informed. Not surprisingly, he felt isolated organizationally and uncertain when called upon to make decisions.

Familiarity with the global organization is critical to effective decision-making. Successful leaders need to know the product lines offered by key subsidiaries; the cost structures and overall competitiveness of key subsidiaries and how these compare to the organization as a whole; and the location and quality of technological resources — both hard assets and people — and of managerial and employee talent within the global organization. Knowing these dimensions gives leaders a better sense of what their organizations can and cannot do.

Lacking familiarity with the global organization, some managers have administrative titles, but they do not lead. They often become resentful when their input is not valued or sought, a particularly acute problem when executives from head office show up once a year as part of an around-the-world junket. Ernie Gundling at Meridian Associates calls this "typhoon management." They come in like a typhoon, mess things up, then go away, leaving the locals to rebuild. In contrast, the most effective global leaders spend at least half their time visiting the "troops in the field." They appreciate that understanding different interests and competencies, although time-consuming and requiring substantial interaction, is valuable.

Mobilizing a global organization's resources also requires that the leader be known by the company's key decision-makers. To develop a high profile within an organization, global leaders must serve on key committees, participate in task forces and attend critical meetings. They must become active participants in two-way communication networks involving head-office and subsidiary decision-makers. It is a mistake to assume that position alone is sufficient to automatically secure these contacts. Substantial personal effort is required.

Skills for Tomorrow's Leaders

Although both global business savvy and organizational savvy are essential competencies for global leaders, they are only the starting points. Global leaders also need unique competencies in relationship management, ethics, making global/local tradeoffs and managing complexity. The knowledge and skills behind these competencies cannot be easily shared with others. To capture the complexities of a global world, tomorrow's leaders must develop a feel for markets, cultures, technologies, values and people. Beyond strategic thinking, having a world view and a drive toward continual learning and personal renewal are demanded of the leader.

U.S. and Canadian leaders must move beyond parochial approaches and simplistic managerial models. A fluid approach to leading in a global organization must be embraced if the gap between global opportunities and the leadership required to pursue them is to be closed.

This article is adapted from the forthcoming book Global Explorers: The Next Generation of Leaders, *by S. Black, A. Morrison and H. Gregersen.*

Rapid Results Yield Stronger Alliances

Douglas Reid

Douglas Reid is a professor of strategy at the School of Business, Queen's University. He is completing a Ph.D. in international business and strategy at the Richard Ivey School of Business.

Alliances are easy to describe but, as many managers have discovered, they demand a unique strategic emphasis for successful implementation. An ongoing Ivey research study is focusing on this question: can managers make smart decisions in the early stages of an alliance's life to begin reaping the benefits of collaboration while minimizing the risks?

Understanding Alliance Dynamics

Whether an equity joint venture or an agreement to collaborate, about half of all cooperative ventures fail due to dissatisfaction expressed by one or more of the partners. The resources that are wasted and the opportunities that are lost are considerable. What is worse, especially for companies first venturing abroad, is the disillusioning effect that premature venture failure has on their future plans for international expansion.

Surprisingly, the causes of failure are remarkably consistent across industries and countries: lack of shared goals; different measures of performance; mixed motives; unrealistic expectations; and underinvestment — both in the time it takes to manage the partner relationship and in delivering the resources needed to make the alliance work.

Initial research findings from a large, multi-year study of alliance dynamics within the international airline industry indicate that managers should pay particular attention to the early stages of an alliance if they wish to increase the chances of long-run success. The study is examining hundreds of alliances formed between the world's leading passenger airlines to identify ways that companies can form good alliances faster. Certain factors and behaviors seem to be associated with more rapid success. Specifically, the initial decisions about partner selection, alliance scope, and the pattern of day-to-day collaboration are emerging as critical differentiators between high- and low-performing alliances.

The idea of speed may contradict what many managers expect about alliances: that the best are the outcome of a deliberative, slow-paced, decision-making process. Yet some firms are able to get good results faster than others, and findings from this research suggest that early positive results contribute significantly to alliance stability and long-term performance.

Most partners decide, usually at the six-month mark, whether an alliance is working or not. That decision, in effect, decides the fate of the alliance because it drives most future partner actions. It is important for managers to achieve results during this early period to allow each side to conclude that initial payoffs are sufficient and future expectations substantial enough to justify continuing the alliance. In alliances, the most important result to managers is a performance improvement that is usually manifested in one of three ways: an increase in revenues; a reduction of costs; or a redeployment of underutilized assets to more productive purposes. And to achieve such results, it is important to do four things:

- properly qualify a partner;
- in the early operational days of the alliance, commit resources incrementally;

- avoid unilateral decisions; and
- consider areas of compromise.

Selecting a Partner

The most time-consuming activities that precede forming an alliance are selecting a partner and negotiating an agreement. Here are some guidelines to consider when selecting a partner.

1. *Find the right differences.* Partners need not be similar in all respects. In fact, it is better to find partners with comparatively distinctive capabilities at different points in the production value chain. These differences should reflect advantages that are attractive to the other partner. They should also represent the potential sources of cost reduction if the superior ability of one partner in managing cost can be transferred to the business of another through collaboration, and vice versa. Another valuable partner difference is their existing access to markets that would otherwise remain closed, or can only be entered at high cost. Moreover, it is important that your prospective partner's advantages be durable, and based on the accumulation and application of either technology or experience in a desirable target market. Understanding the nature, extent and potential value of partner differences cannot be overemphasized because they create the rationale for the alliance in the first place, and form the basis for negotiations about alliance terms.
2. *Find the right similarities.* Collaborators from the same industry have the advantage of understanding each other's business. They also understand the costs and risks entailed with the ongoing commitment of tangible resources (valuable activities, services or goods) as well as intangible resources (reputation or brand name) to a collaborative venture.

   And while there must be key overlaps in some parts of the product value chain or in respective geographic markets served, other similarities are key to producing positive results in the early months of an alliance. For example, compatible corporate cultures make it easier to establish effective working relationships from the start, since jointly held norms about decision-making processes and information-sharing, for example, minimize friction and facilitate getting things done. In the global airline industry, one of the key reasons cited for particular partner selection decisions was the anticipated compatibility of corporate cultures. The consequences of this finding are relevant to companies everywhere: screening first by compatibility reduces the number of prospective partners and makes the search process more efficient. One executive from a large U.S. airline put it succinctly: "There may be lots of carriers in this country, but there are only two that we'd even think of working with, because we all have the same style."

3. *Find a common positioning to customers.* Markets are segmented and so are airlines. Travelers tend to group carriers based on the carriers' operating characteristics and product quality, and cluster them with others that have a similar reputation. Two companies with similar reputations will, all things being equal, collaborate more effectively than two companies that customers hold in substantially different levels of esteem.

The reason is straightforward: transparency to the customer. A European executive, when describing the good relationships his company enjoyed with a North American airline, noted that one of the key factors that confirmed early success was passenger satisfaction: "When our passengers were flying on our partner's plane, they didn't notice any difference in quality at all. That's what they were expecting."

Companies that ally outside their segment, even for the straightforward purpose of gaining access to valuable routes, must take action to ensure alignment between their product and operating characteristics and those of their partner. That means either having to insist on potentially costly changes to the partner carrier's product/service mix or shouldering the cost of those changes to rise to the partner's standard.

While differences in the products or operating characteristics of prospective partners are to be expected, they should not be so divergent as to create a situation in which one partner benefits more than the other from knowledge-sharing. Partnerships are supposed to be examples of win-win relationships. Unbalanced exchanges tend to be short-lived exchanges.

4. *Find the yardstick for success.* Surprisingly, few executives in the study had a clear understanding of the measures that their partners were using to evaluate the alliance. While it is important for a management team to be internally cohesive on key measures of success, not being aware of a partner's critical success factors is dangerous to alliance stability. This lack of understanding creates the risk that your actions may unintentionally obstruct your partner's goals. Although partner success criteria are usually discovered as an alliance evolves, it can often be too late. Furthermore, clarifying your prospective partner's criteria early on allows you to decide whether you can collaborate effectively. If not, perhaps it makes sense to consider another partner.

An executive from a European carrier involved in a short-lived alliance summarized the measurement dilemma succinctly: "At the six-month mark, we sat down with our partner to compare notes. Based on our measures, we were ready to continue working together, but it turned out that the partner wasn't happy. We were worried about revenues; they were worried about load factor [use of aircraft capacity]. It became clear we couldn't continue without substantial changes."

Operating to Succeed

Once a partner has been selected, it is important to consider that the actions taken by both partners can enhance the chances of alliance survival in the critical short term. Here, two considerations matter most:

1. *Commit resources incrementally.* Once the scope of the alliance has been decided, most key decisions involve the commitment of additional resources. To enhance the chances of success, in general, these resources should be committed in small increments at frequent intervals. Compared with the principal alternative — large increments at infrequent intervals — frequent

resource commitments send an important signal to a partner about the value you place on the alliance. And consistent with other research, partner commitment is signaled most strongly by sequential rather than coincident resource commitments.

2. *Understand the effect of unilateral decisions on the alliance.* Unilateral decisions have bilateral impacts. The ability to change from the usual managerial mindset in which unilateral action is common in a competitive context to one that considers partner reactions in a collaborative context is strongly associated with alliance durability and improved performance. For example, one partner may cut the price of a service they are selling that happens to be delivered through the partnership. While the business rationale for doing so may be entirely logical, this decision can, in effect, place the partners in a more acute competitive position with each other. An example of a now-defunct operating alliance between U.S. and South American carriers emphasizes this point well. According to one U.S. executive: "Without telling us, our South American partner dropped the price of their seats on a flight we were operating. When travel agents heard of this, they rebooked many of our ticket holders through our partner, got the lower fare, and took a lot of revenue from us." His South American counterpart had a different perspective: "We did what we had to do to fill our half of the airplane. We thought the Americans would understand." It's important to take the time to make the right decisions with your partner and strengthen the alliance in the process.

3. *How partners coordinate.* Getting things done better, faster, or at lower cost is the purpose behind forming an alliance in the first place. This happens through the processes of exchange and coordination. In exchange, partners trade knowledge or technology within the context of a shared production agreement. Such trading comes about only through effective coordination. Coordination usually takes place in two ways: first, through day-to-day contacts between operational managers who share information and resolve operational problems; and second, through coordinating committees that collaborate on the joint management of the alliance. The best-performing

alliances reach a balance between the two forms of coordination by ensuring the operational managers have the authority and resources to collaborate, and by structuring the alliance relationship so that operational contacts occur at many levels within each partner company. The coordinating committee is used often in the early days of the alliance to solve problems, address questions of short-term strategy and enable companies to learn more about the preferences of their partners. In the best alliances, problems rarely escalate to senior management levels for ultimate resolution, and the contract between the partners is used as a starting point for negotiations rather than a finishing point. If a company cannot commit to this type of operational style, either due to reasons of corporate culture or the scarcity of management resources, it reduces its chances of performing successfully.

Alliances aren't the solution for every company, nor does every company make an effective alliance partner. However, those companies that are able to foresee the opportunities presented by collaboration and take action to seize those opportunities before their competitors do, will be the ones that succeed fastest in an increasingly interconnected global economy. Careful attention to the partner selection process and the operational implementation of the alliance can improve the likelihood of realizing the early successes needed to justify continuation.

Considering Alliances?
Consider These Questions:

- What are my company's strengths compared to my partner's?
- What are the strengths of my prospective partner? Where are the similarities and differences?
- If we could exchange skills, which ones do we value most? Would it be a fair exchange?
- What shared markets do we serve? Where do we differ?
- How important are their markets to us and vice versa?
- How similar are our corporate cultures?
- What similarities do our products share? What are the key differences?
- Can products be improved by drawing on our partner's skills?
- What are we prepared to invest to align our product performance with theirs?
- How important is an alliance to my company's success?
- Do our managers have the time and resources to work effectively within an alliance?
- What are our partner's criteria for success? Can we live with those criteria?
- How do their criteria affect the chances of realizing our goals?

V
Competing in the Americas

Assessing the Risks for Competitive Advantage in Latin America

David W. Conklin

David W. Conklin is a professor of international strategy at the Richard Ivey School of Business.

For decades, a high degree of political risk has discouraged foreign investment in Latin America. But recent years have witnessed major changes in the nature and extent of Latin American country risks, including a dramatic reduction in political risks, and an increase in economic ones. At the same time, there has been a vast opening up of investment opportunities, and Canadian corporations are transferring modern technology and business practices that exceed the capabilities of domestic corporations, creating country- and industry-specific competitive advantages.

Political Risks

Prior to 1990, the political risks associated with interventionist governments were considerable, and included a high probability of government expro-priation, detailed regulations that imposed inefficiencies, and restrictions on foreign investment. The goal of economic self-suffi-ciency supported extensive tariff and nontariff barriers to both trade and investment. Further, bribery often influenced government invest-ment approvals. Today, however, such political risk has been replaced by a faith in free markets, and an acceptance that international trade and investment are the bases for economic growth.

Certainly, Latin America's extreme polarization of income and wealth will not always fit comfortably with a new faith in democracy. As such, there is a possibility that arbitrary government intervention may occur, and investors should remain cautious. For example, the effects of the 1993 election of the president of Venezuela, Rafael Caldera — a supporter of an interventionist role for government in the 1970s — and the 1996 election of the president of Ecuador, Abdul Bucaram — who promised extensive government assistance for the poor and who was later overthrown by a coup of the elite within a few months of his electoral victory — indicate that political risk must still be an element of the investment decision.

For natural resource sectors in particular, political risk may still be a "show stopper" — where the risk of nationalization, special taxes or new regulations is particularly severe. Managers in these sectors must consider whether the risks may be too high to justify investment. It remains necessary to heed the views of local political experts. One technique involves circulating a questionnaire to these experts, compiling the results, and returning the results to the respondents for further commentary. This "Delphi" technique facilitates the develop-ment of a consensus view on those risks that a potential investor faces.

Interestingly, political risk has diminished in Latin America at the same time that it has escalated in Canada. Inco's experience with the Voisey Bay delays as a result of environmental objections, the advocacy of aboriginal rights and the issue of government taxes, for example, has caused considerable difficulties compared with the relatively easy approval processes for mining in Latin American countries. When the question of Quebec's secession is added to these political risks, many Canadian corporations may conclude that such risks in Canada exceed those in Latin America, and that, in this respect, Latin America offers a competitive advantage. However, other country risks have come to occupy center stage in Latin American investment decisions.

Economic Risks

Traditional investments in natural resources by foreign investors were supplemented in the 1960s by loans to foreign governments and, more recently, by purchases of stocks in Latin American corporations. With these investments, the risk of foreign exchange rate movements has become a paramount consideration, as has the risk that the government may simply lack the economic capacity to repay loans. The devaluation cycle remains a key economic risk in Latin America. Many Latin American countries have been experiencing ongoing fiscal deficits, and money supply growth that exceeds that of each of the United States, Canada, and Western Europe. Consequently, inflation rates remain high. And the realities of exchange rates mean that devaluation crises will appear from time to time. Managers should prepare themselves accordingly, with an analysis of interest rates and stock prices, the country's balance of payments, projections of probable macroeconomic policies and fiscal and current account deficits. Organizations like the Economist Intelligence Unit now assign risk rankings to each country based upon such analyses. It is important to examine alternative potential scenarios and projections, and assign probabilities to each scenario in order to determine the risks and rewards connected with particular investment opportunities.

But how can foreign investors protect themselves from these economic risks? Hedging mechanisms offer some hope for reducing foreign exchange risks, but generally not without some cost. Here are some other ways managers can cope with the economic risks of the Latin American region:

1. *Consider the timing of your investments.* Investors should restrict capital transfers into a country to those times when the foreign exchange rate is in equilibrium. Labatt signed an agreement with Femsa, a Mexican beer producer, just prior to the 1994 peso crisis, resulting in a substantial fall in the Canadian dollar value of the investment.
2. *Borrow domestically to do business domestically* and avoid foreign exchange rate exposure. Keep in mind that this approach does expose the business to the possibility of interest rate increases, as a result of a central bank's response to foreign

exchange rate devaluation. For a foreign-owned financial institution, this approach also involves the possibility of a "run" on deposits, as the depositors seek to withdraw funds in order to transfer them abroad.

3. *Focus on the devaluation risk* when choosing among countries as investment sites. For example, Chile is currently a less risky region for investment than Argentina or Mexico.

4. *Consider the amount of capital required* by those activities that are being developed in a country subject to devaluation risk. The significance of a foreign exchange risk may be relatively low for a business that requires little capital investment, like the service sector or fast food industry, or high for a firm in the manufacturing and natural resource sectors, where the capital required is considerable.

5. *Spread the purchase price* over as long a time period as possible. This allows domestic currency to be purchased at a lower cost if devaluation occurs. Alternatively, gear the purchase price to a weighted average of the exchange rate over future years, with projected future payments adjusted in accordance with the exchange rate.

Domestic Competitive Advantage

In recent years, foreign corporations have begun to invest in Latin America for the purpose of generating sales within the domestic economies of the region. Growth rates have reached their highest level in decades, and offer the promise of rapidly expanding consumer and business purchases. In addition to considering political and economic risks, managers must analyze the domestic situation for such industry risks as the strength of competitors, the potential for substitutes, the capabilities of suppliers and customers, and the risk of other new entrants. It may be helpful to determine risk level by developing a matrix in which each industry risk is evaluated as minor, serious, or "show stopping," and in which the various ways of mitigating each risk are analyzed. For many foreign corporations, an example of industry risk may be the difficulty of finding suppliers who can offer the required level of quality and service. Public utility disruptions may also be risky, especially for firms dealing in perishable commodities —

in some countries, for example, electricity outages are common. For some Canadian corporations, one solution has been to encourage other Canadian or U.S. suppliers to open a business in the same locality. For others, the construction of one's own utilities, such as power supply, is a solution to the risk of electricity outages. Such actions may serve to strengthen a corporation's domestic competitive advantage. Further, the process of developing a matrix of industry risks leads to strategies and solutions unique to each country, and indeed, to regions within countries as well.

Opportunities abound for foreign corporations to enjoy a competitive advantage in Latin America, as many of the region's industries have failed to keep up with the advances in business practices and technologies of the past 50 years. Compared with Canada, the age profile is substantially younger in many Latin American countries. And as the North American consumption pattern forms the ideal which many young Latin American people follow, the products and services that foreign corporations are developing can find a ready market within the younger age group living in the rapidly growing urban centers of the region.

Widespread privatization is also offering further opportunities to do business in Latin American markets. It was the privatization of Argentina's government-owned oil and gas business, for example, that gave Chauvco Resources Ltd. an initial investment opportunity in Latin America. And today, the privatization of government-owned banks offers foreign banks similar opportunities.

International Competitive Advantage

Corporations are increasingly developing geographically integrated, global production and distribution systems in order to remain competitive. The multinational enterprise seeks to specialize in those elements of the value chain that can be most effectively produced in each foreign country. The automobile industry provides an example where a multitude of components are sourced from a number of countries, but assembled in one location. Indeed, success depends on the ability to innovate continually and to modify products and services to suit the customer's needs. However, investing in Latin American countries for international sourcing of products and components means accepting the risks of a diminishing international competitive advantage. In general, these countries do not yet possess the capabilities to support continual innovation and cost reductions.

It will always be necessary for managers to consider a country's competitiveness factors when making investment decisions. Latin American countries continue to rank poorly in international surveys of such factors. Consequently, labor-intensive export facilities, for example, are more likely to be located in other regions of the world, despite Latin America's lower wage levels. Findings in the *World Competitiveness Yearbook* provide some critical data on the competitiveness factors of 46 countries, where a number of Latin American countries currently rank low on the scale — Mexico, for example, has been ranked 40th in such competitiveness factors as its domestic economy, its degree of internationalization, finance, science and technology, and human resource capabilities. Although Colombia, Argentina, Brazil, and Venezuela also hold a currently low ranking, Chile stands as a sharp contrast — it ranks 10th in the world for its domestic economy and government, and 20th for its competitiveness factors.

Managers would do well to consider each Latin American region independently. Many countries contain a high-growth region with strong competitive attributes. For example, Mexico's U.S. border region and Monterrey are often regarded as a part of the U.S. economy rather than the Mexican economy, since a major portion of trade and investment is cross-border. As such, many corporate global strategies involve placing considerable investments in specific Latin American regions.

As we enter the next century, Latin America continues to emerge as a formidable global player and holds considerable potential as an investment site. Many corporations are taking advantage of the competitive opportunities opening up in the region. But before doing business in Latin America, managers must carefully analyze the political and economic risks involved, and establish provisions for coping with them in order to reach their best chances for success.

Latin America: Flourishing with Emerging Markets

Ken Clark

Ken Clark is managing director of 3M Chile and a graduate of Ivey's MBA program.

D ramatic economic reforms have opened the door for equally dramatic business opportunities in Latin America. Yet these opportunities do not fall in equal measure to all players. The lessons in Latin America are clear: while ours is evermore a global economy, size is no guarantor of success. Equally powerful forces pull us toward local realities that demand different responses. Managing this contradiction well involves being able to adapt, and that is the cornerstone lesson for firms with global aspirations. Without "street-smart" tactics, strategy is merely design.

The size and scale of change are stunning in Latin America. Driven by the dramatic success of Chile's structural reforms more than a decade ago, and by the final recognition of their uncompetitive position, neighboring countries enacted liberalizing market reforms with haste. The Mexican and Argentinean currency crises strengthened rather than broke the financial discipline of their nations. Last year local economies grew in the 5 percent range, led by Argentina and Peru at 8 percent. With inflation in single digits in all but a few countries, imports surged to US$210 billion from 1990 to 1996. From opportunity flowed return, and foreign investments grew 52 percent between 1995 and 1996.

Typical of emerging economies, activity in Latin American infrastructure is surging. Telecommunications, construction, energy and other primary industries are advancing dramatically. While poverty and social mobility remain undeniable challenges of the region, millions of people have felt the effects of real income gains, and the result is a dynamic retail sector. Sales of savvy retailers have grown between 50 and 100 percent — Wal-Mart alone experienced 400 percent sales growth in Argentina in 1996. And some markets have achieved levels of sophistication rivaling anywhere in the world — Chileans enjoy one of the world's most advanced telecommunications networks and some of the lowest long-distance rates.

Indeed, these are not sleepy markets, nor is such phenomenal growth easy to achieve. The business landscape is becoming crowded — global transnationals, who call Europe, Asia and North America home, are becoming well entrenched. The European position has proven strong in privatizations. Telefonica de España has created a powerhouse operation in the Latin American region by gobbling up telephone companies in Chile, Peru and Argentina. The transnationals are also having to compete with the emergence of powerful local firms. These companies are involved in everything from food and beer to cement and airlines. Popularly called the "Multi Latinas," they are not yet global but are bursting forth from their local countries and are quickly becoming strong regional enterprises. These companies are strong — they are on their own playing field, and have the necessary business and political connections to do business successfully. As such, they operate with greater ease in the Latin American business environment.

This commingling of global and local firms gives cause for thoughtful strategy, but more challenging yet is the lack of homogeneity among countries. This makes a single regional strategy almost out of the question. As the level of Latin American modernity still trails the developed economies of the world, major differences continue to exist between countries. Argentina leads the way with a GDP per capita of almost US$10,000, but this amount trails off quickly, totaling a mere $1,000 per person for countries such as land-locked Bolivia. Brazil's economy of some US$770 billion, now one of the world's largest, dwarfs Chile's US$75 billion economy, which itself is 10 times larger than that of neighboring Bolivia. Protectionist tariffs and less explicit barriers make interregional transportation challenging. Further, no clear regional center has yet emerged — in fact, Miami is often the default location for Latin American headquarters.

The final dimension of regional differentiation — culture — is the most interesting and, at the same time, the most challenging. Tactics set in motion the grand design that strategy implies, and how a plan is implemented on the ground by real people in real environments becomes, for some companies, a barrier that is never overcome. Those who understand local market realities can achieve lockout competitive positions. The area is deeply rooted in family and tradition — perhaps more so than Europe or North America. Class distinctions and deference to authority are common. Where American organizations have spent the past decade building less structured companies that spread power deep into the organization, the typical Latin American organization prefers to operate with a clear and defined hierarchical structure. And although this is changing, it has significant implications at the operational level. For example, where global accounts call for sophisticated key account skills, enormous responsibility rests with the customer interface — the sales professional. Such a role is not seen in the same light as other management positions in Latin America (indeed the title "sales representative" is often a barrier to account development), and as such, recruiting, training and retaining a capable professional sales force is a considerable challenge.

Although macroeconomic realities translate into growth and opportunity, issues such as culture and taste indicate specific "real world" market conditions. Any marketer plotting country-specific market size or segmentation based on prior experience may be making incorrect assumptions. One example is found in the home improvement market. North American socioeconomic realities have produced a generation of weekend do-it-yourselfers. However, in Latin America, the combination of lower wages, different home ownership rates and differing perceptions of social status implicit in performing such work yourself, produces a different market dynamic. And hardware manufacturers or distributors need to respond accordingly.

Successful firms must know where and when to leverage power and scale where appropriate and when to play the "street savvy" card. Coca-Cola's global brand is buttressed with an equally powerful local bottler network. Coke's share in Latin America, notwithstanding Peru's Inca Kola, represents its strongest share position worldwide. In a flat Brazilian car market, sales of Fiat's first international platform car, the Palio, grew 150 percent to US$850 million. Well-positioned firms are reaping the rewards of this market by not only understanding the size of the opportunity but, equally as important, how to operationalize it on the ground. The ability to find and retain key regional partners is an important way to achieve a dominant position.

3M has operations in virtually every country in Latin America and some of its subsidiaries are among the company's oldest. Perhaps owing to the enormous complexity of the company and with it the need to learn the importance of balance, 3M has managed its success in Latin America well. Local subsidiaries are empowered with well-trained nationals who focus on the global vision; the subsidiaries alone are responsible for their own back yard and build their own local growth platforms. Headquarters-based product groups with divisional targets take technology and products to the subsidiaries. Although the climate, at times, is one of creative disharmony, it is the local, on-the-ground capability that enables innovation to move from the laboratory to the customer. There are presently a number of such centers of excellence in the textiles, automotive, petroleum and mining industries. Employees throughout the area are encouraged to be as innovative in their approaches to business as are the scientists. Certainly, anything less would not keep 3M competitive.

As opportunities continue to emerge in Latin America, larger firms are creating organizations with regional strengths. Indeed, few firms with global aspirations can ignore the Latin American economy — and local firms cannot avoid it. Success will come sooner and in larger measure to those who can balance global strengths with the heterogeneity that local markets demand.

Understanding the Language of Business in Latin America

Claude Lanfranconi and Dan Campbell

Claude Lanfranconi is a professor of accounting at the Richard Ivey School of Business. Dan Campbell is the former director of Ivey's Program Mexico and an Ivey HBA graduate.

If you want to do business in Latin America, you have a little more to learn after mastering *Como esta usted*. After learning the Spanish language, you must then learn to speak the language of business: accounting. While the Americas encompass a region as diverse as any in the world, there is one element shared by virtually every nation south of the Rio Grande: inflation. And the language of business needed to manage in an inflationary environment demands its own unique "dialect."

Although the region's history of bouts with four-digit general price increases seems to have temporarily subsided, the 1995 meltdown of the Mexican economy later echoed in 1997, as pressure mounted

[175]

against Brazil's currency. This serves as a continuing reminder that the health of these economies and currencies remains tenuous at best. Only recently have general rates of inflation dropped below 10 percent, and only in the strongest economies of the region.

Since financial reports use a monetary unit of measurement, substantial changes in price levels have a significant impact on the financial data typically used to measure business performance. This impedes not only potential investors and their analysts as they attempt to evaluate the firm, but also managers of the firm who need such information upon which to base their daily decisions. As a result, alternative methods of accounting have been developed and are used to adjust for changing prices over time. These provide a more relevant financial measure of a firm's activities.

Mexico: A Sophisticated Example

Of all the inflation accounting systems used throughout Latin America, Mexico's is by far the most sophisticated. The basic elements of inflation accounting are similar throughout the region — and becoming familiar with Mexico's accounting methods is a good place to start.

When using Mexican financial statements, it is important to recognize that they reflect an attempt to portray the economic reality of a highly inflationary economy with a history of currency devaluations. U.S. and Canadian inflation has, for the most part, been gradual. There are in fact many similarities in Mexico and its NAFTA partners' financial accounting practices, but there are also a number of differences. Accounting for inflation is the most significant visible difference between Mexican and U.S. or Canadian financial statements. Canadian and U.S. financial statements are primarily cost-based, whereas Mexican statements are adjusted for both general and specific price changes. These adjustments characterize financial statements prepared by companies in Mexico and other countries that have experienced significant continuous inflation, such as Argentina, Brazil and Chile. In fact, without these adjustments a statement's usefulness is greatly diminished.

Separating the Effects of Changing Prices

The approach taken by those who establish Mexican accounting standards is both comprehensive and technically advanced. The Mexican Institute of Public Accountants Bulletin B-10 requires companies to adjust for both general (constant pesos) and specific price changes, temporary overvaluations of the local currency relative to foreign currencies, and the restatement of comparative financial data, in terms of the general purchasing power stated on the most recent balance sheet.

As a result, and despite the potential for significant distortion resulting from inflation and its impact on the purchasing power of the peso, inflation-adjusted Mexican financial statements can be used to perform financial analysis and comparisons over time similar to what one might do with U.S. and Canadian statements. Further, Mexican financial statements can be used to better evaluate how well companies are coping with the impact of inflation on their operations. For example, a financial analyst might assess a company on a number of critical dimensions: how well the company manages its cash, including the maintenance of its purchasing power; the measurement of real growth; and the evaluation of real performance. Without these general price level and specific adjustments, it would be difficult to separate the effects of inflation from real growth resulting from decisions taken by the firm's management, or to ascertain if the company's increased gross margin is due to inflation or good management.

Because of the inflationary environment in which Latin American companies operate, inflation-adjusted data are critical if one is to be able to determine nominal growth — which is affected by inflation — from real growth. Some might argue that the problem is the lack of adjustments in Canada and the United States, where inflation has, over time, distorted the dollar-measuring stick. Defenders of the current system in Canada and the United States argue that the distortion is not so severe and that the additional data has limited use.

Over the years, Canadian and U.S. accountants have experimented with adjustments for changing prices. In 1979, the Financial Accounting Standards Board (FASB) issued Financial Accounting Standard No. 33, "Financial Reporting and Changing Prices." It was subsequently made voluntary in 1986. In 1982, the Canadian

Accounting Standards Committee (AcSC — now the Accounting Standards Board) introduced section 4510 to the Canadian Institute of Chartered Accountants (CICA) handbook, outlining the recommendation that large, publicly held companies voluntarily present certain minimum information about the effects of changing prices together with their annual historic cost-based financial statements. But as inflation rates declined, so too did interest in accounting for changing prices — and, by March 1992, the AcSC withdrew these recommendations from the CICA handbook.

Using Financial Reports

If the only difference between Canadian, U.S., and Mexican financial reporting is accounting for changing prices, it might be argued by those in favor of these adjustments that Mexican statements are a better reflection of economic reality. They would argue that comparisons over time are more realistic with adjustments of the currency for price changes. But changes in the value of the Canadian and U.S. dollars, which has declined over time, are not yet reflected in their financial reporting.

If an individual is already a reasonably knowledgeable user of corporate financial reports, the next step of using non-national financial statements is not insurmountable. Frequently, English-language reports are available. They often look like U.S. and Canadian financial statements, use similar terminology, and are frequently audited by international auditing firms. However, be careful not to assume that they are fully comparable to U.S. and Canadian financial statements. Although there are many similarities, common accounting terms and methods, such as goodwill and its amortization, the selection of which practices are used or permitted in a particular jurisdiction, and how they are implemented, may be different. Over what period of time is the goodwill to be amortized, five, 10, 40 years — or should it be completely written off at the date of acquisition? Therefore, together with an adequate financial accounting background in using financial statements generally and some careful reading, a manager should be able to apply that knowledge and, after a few adjustments, cope with many of the differences found in non-national financial statements.

If a foreign company trades on a U.S. stock exchange, for example, or issues securities in the United States, adjustments and analysis of

Mexican statements are made easier. Mexican companies that trade securities in the United States are mandated to file a 20-F form with the Securities and Exchange Commission (SEC), requiring considerable additional information and a reconciliation of their statements to U.S. standards. The form is the foreign equivalent of a 10-K, and requires companies to provide financial information about the company, such as financial statements and their content. However, foreign companies that file reports using their domestic financial statements are required to reconcile earnings to the policies outlined by the U.S. Generally Accepted Accounting Principles (GAAP). These filings are publicly available, directly from the SEC or through its EDGAR database. And combined with the similarity between Canadian and U.S. GAAP, an understanding of Mexican financial statements by domestic analysts is made considerably easier.

There are extensive financial data available to interested users, sometimes translated into English, which might also be reconciled to U.S. GAAP. What is needed is knowledge of the common significant differences, patience to carefully review a company's accounting policies for other, less common differences, and a willingness to use data which are sufficient to meet user needs — even if they are not completely similar to those found in U.S. or Canadian financial statements.

The same advice applies to those users of Latin American financial data as to those of financial data in general: be educated skeptics. Combine your current knowledge of financial reporting with a familiarity of the nature of inflation adjustments. Rather than be an impediment to understanding, such adjustments may be just the right medicine to help you cope with a "sick" monetary measurement.

The principal features of the Mexican GAAP for inflation according to the Mexican Institute of Public Accountants Bulletin (B-10):

- As opposed to historical cost-based financial statements, property and equipment, as well as construction-in-progress, are restated to their current cost using the specific cost method.
- Depreciation is based on the current cost of the related assets.
- The specific cost method is used to measure inventories and their related cost-of-goods sold expense.
- The company's net purchasing power gains or losses on monetary items are measured and included in the determination of the company's total financing costs.
- All financial statements are stated in pesos of purchasing power at the close of the most recent period.
- Comparative prior period financial statements are restated to the purchasing power equivalent of the peso at the close of the most recent period — the last month of the current financial statement.
- There is also an adjustment for those situations where, for a variety of reasons, the Mexican peso is overvalued relative to the U.S. dollar.

Connecting Latin America . . . and the World

David Winfield

David Winfield, a former Cana-
dian trade commissioner and
formerly Canada's ambassador to
Mexico, became the senior vice-
president, government relations
for Nortel in 1995. He is a
former participant of Ivey's inter-
national management executive
development program.★

Take Latin America, a region of emerging — and in Brazil's case, re-emerging — markets, add a global information revolution and a company that must grow international sales, and you have the makings of a truly complementary and successful business venture. Nortel (Northern Telecom) — the Canadian-based multinational that started business in Montreal more than 100 years ago, and a leading

★ *This article appeared in the "Competing in the Americas" issue of* Managing for Success *in* The Globe and Mail *on February 13, 1998. The facts and statistics noted in this article reflect the status of Nortel and the surrounding economic conditions taking place at that time.*

provider of digital network solutions — saw the opportunities in, and importance of, this region more than 20 years ago. Following some simple rules that apply to doing business in just about any international market, Nortel has become a leading supplier of communications networks to the countries of Latin America, and is an active participant in the development of other economies. A strong and impressive future is expected for this region through the increased deregulation of telecommunications — and other sectors — and the opening up to foreign investors of new and promising markets.

In the early 1960s, Nortel began building its presence in the Caribbean. Here it learned the importance of treating each country as a separate market, and that, to do business successfully, respecting the different cultures and languages was as essential as understanding each country's unique telecommunications needs. Nortel was quick to apply these lessons throughout Latin America.

In 1975, Nortel CALA (Caribbean and Latin America) opened its head office in Florida under the direction of Northern Telecom Canada. By 1992, CALA had grown to such a degree that it was spun off as a separate entity, reporting to Northern Telecom Limited. It has become one of the company's fastest-growing business units, with revenues increasing from US$200 million in 1990 to more than $1 billion in 1997. Currently, sales occur in all 47 countries of the region, and the company has offices and personnel in such countries as Brazil, Mexico, Colombia, Argentina, Chile, Puerto Rico and Peru.

Several factors instigated Nortel's recent decision to focus more attention and resources on the region, including:

- *A need for improved telecommunications capabilities.* Most countries in the region have less than 10 phone lines per 100 people — and some have less than five. The various governments of Latin America are strongly committed to expanding the region's phone line capacity.
- *Privatization, deregulation and spectrum allocation.* Serious privatization of government-owned telcos started in the late 1980s, opening markets to a host of both local and multinational investors. For example, the administration under Mexican President Carlos Salinas de Gortari attempted to privatize 70

percent of the state's enterprises, including the state telecommunications company, Telmex. Because of deregulation and the resulting surge in competition in wireless and long-distance services, Nortel has been able to capture a significant portion of the Mexican market. Moreover, in 1996, Nortel built the first new long-distance network in Mexico for the newly licenced alternative carrier, Avantel — a joint venture between MCI and Banamex.

- *Support through the Department of Foreign Affairs and International Trade (DFAIT), Canadian embassies and trade offices.* Canadian embassies and trade offices throughout the region offer a variety of services to help Canadian exporters get established in the marketplace. The Caribbean and Latin American branch of DFAIT has offices across Canada that provide useful information and counsel to fledgling and experienced exporters on the various marketplaces, how to do business in these markets, and the range of contacts exporters require.
- *Export Development Corporation (EDC) and bank support.* The EDC provides export financing and repayment insurance, while a variety of financial services for exporters and investors are provided by the Canadian chartered banks through representative offices throughout the region. For example, Bank of Montreal and Scotiabank have ownership positions in banks based in Mexico.

In addition, the dramatic changes that have taken place over the past decade have substantially changed the environment for foreign companies wishing to do business in Latin America. Democratically elected governments have been established, market economies have emerged — opening markets previously closed to foreign companies. And of equal importance, most markets treat foreign companies on par with local investors. All economies, except Cuba, are members of the World Trade Organization and have accordingly accepted the multilateral rules-based trading system. Further, they have implemented or are committed to implementing clearer rules for foreign investment. The acceptance of both basic tenets is very important in attracting new foreign investment, resulting in job creation and technology transfer.

The nations of the region have embarked on a determined program to integrate economically and establish free trade zones, and dozens of trade agreements have already been adopted. The North American Free Trade Agreement (NAFTA) is an important example to the region of the benefits of free trade. Mercosur creates a free trade association between Brazil, Argentina, Uruguay and Paraguay, the "Common Market of the South" — with Bolivia and Chile on the verge of membership. There has been aggressive reduction — and in some cases, elimination — of tariff and nontariff barriers.

And dramatic changes continue to take place. Analysts expect full integration of the Mercosur countries to occur some time after 2001. In addition, the heads of all of the democratically elected nations of the Americas continue to prepare for the negotiations of the Free Trade Area of the Americas (FTAA) — a process started in December 1994 at the Summit of the Americas — which is expected to be implemented by the year 2005.

The region has also seen growth in fiscal responsibility, a reduction in government spending and deficits, the elimination of excessive inflation, and the establishment of clear-cut management, including more independent central banks.

All of these changes have attracted new investment and have resulted in powerful economic growth contributing to the modernization of the countries' infrastructures, and expansion in such areas as mining, agroindustry, energy, transportation, tourism and telecommunications. Further, with more open markets, there have been rising demands and expectations by consumers for better quality and variety of goods and services — at better prices. These changes, along with continued advances in technology, represent opportunities and challenges for Nortel and for other Canadian investors and exporters.

Saying that all is perfect in Latin America would be incorrect — much work remains to be done. Judicial systems need to be reformed; the continuing high rates of crime and narcotics trafficking need to be combatted. Improvements need to be made in education and job training, and efforts to reduce and eventually eliminate poverty must continue.

However, the region is more politically stable than ever before, and its economies are growing. In fact, Latin America is relatively free from some of the more extreme types of religious and border conflicts that exist in other parts of the world.

Telecommunications

The growth in the telecoms sector illustrates the dynamism and vitality of the revolutionary changes that are taking place in our own hemisphere. In her book *The Post–Cold War Trading System: Who's on First?*, former Canadian ambassador to the Uruguay Round of GATT Sylvia Ostry stated that of the changes that have taken place in the world economy since the Second World War, it is the evolution in communication technology that has been the main driver behind the opening of markets and the move toward a globalized economy. And in Latin America in particular, according to Matt Desch, president of Nortel's wireless networks, "While there was relative political stability and leadership occurring in Latin America, technology came up with something called wireless cellular telephones, replacing two-way mobiles. …The wireless business is important in Latin America because you don't have to take dishes, lay cable, add transmissions, build towers and design a radio frequency network. Wireless allows the quick deployment of dial tone to as many users as possible, very cost effectively."

The transformation that has affected the telecommunications sector mirrors the changes in thinking about national economies that have taken place in such countries as Mexico and Chile — that is, let the market decide. In turn, new players and investors have been stimulated into entering the market, creating global supercarriers with alliances between companies such as British Telecom, MCI, AT&T, Deutsche-Bundespost and others. This has lead to investment in new networks by incumbents and new operators; the introduction of new technology, new jobs, and better service for customers; and education and training in engineering, computer science and other, related fields. Nortel is a supplier to many major supercarriers, as well as a leading supplier to the world's cable and wireless companies.

The telecommunications sector will continue to grow. Annual investment in telecommunications through the region is expected to grow by many billions of dollars a year by the year 2000. Brazil alone is expected to spend US$100 billion on telecommunications between 1995 and 2000. The results will be a proliferation of new operators and wireless networks, as well as the growth of private networks and the rapid expansion of data traffic throughout the area.

Winfield's Five Golden Rules

Nortel's success in Latin America can be attributed to the following — what I refer to as the "five golden rules" for successful international business:

1. *Remember that you are not alone.* The federal trade service and their trade offices in embassies around the world are available to help, as are the Canadian chartered banks, with offices located in most countries of the region. The EDC provides export financing and repayment guarantees. Lawyers and chartered accountants are other sources of information and guidance. And don't forget that the Internet also has a huge amount of data on a country and sector basis.
2. *Research is vital.* Learn all you can about the marketplace, the history of the region and the culture — especially the business culture — before you visit. Learn all you can about your sector, the conditions for doing business there, and what the competition is doing.
3. *Develop a plan of action* or strategy and determine which of the following mechanisms would work best for you: direct sales, agency/distributor, licencee (manufacturing and technology), partnership (which would need to be well defined and understood) or a wholly owned subsidiary.
4. *Build relations first; do business second.* Relationships are the most important aspect of doing business successfully in the international arena. Be patient. Spend time getting to know your business partners. Try to learn about their culture and language, and try not to impose your way of doing business. In Mexico, 95 percent of Nortel's staff is Mexican, and there are similar statistics in Brazil, where the company has a Brazilian president. An enormous amount of energy has been spent recruiting the right people with the right qualifications so that we speak the language of the customer — both literally and figuratively. Indeed, with Nortel's employment of

local staff for the plants and offices, and the appointing of local general managers and executives, we are becoming Mexican in Mexico, Brazilian in Brazil, Colombian in Colombia — and this applies to every region in which we operate.

5. *Do not break the law.* Avoid falling prey to the fallacy that in order to do business you have to pay bribes. In all countries it is illegal and it is a practice that cannot be condoned. Nortel has followed these rules and has demonstrated its commitment to Latin America by building a strong presence with local resources.

For Nortel, the ability to access international markets is the key to its success as a company, affecting not only Latin American markets, but its home market as well. As former president and CEO, Jean Monty, stated: "Without its commitment to globalization, Nortel would lose its vitality and stop being a global resource to its Canadian customers and a constructive element of Canada's economic development."

Latin America has offered Nortel a diverse region in which to do business. While the varying needs throughout the region's nations could have spelled difficulty for a company focused on offering one solution, Nortel has chosen to meet these challenges with unique answers while still offering integration between the various countries' systems and those of the rest of the world. After all, globalization — in any industry — can't occur until the world is connected.

Examples of Nortel's Work in Latin America

The Latin American region is rapidly privatizing and deregulating its telecommunications industry. Nortel has been instrumental in supporting operators entering this new era of competition and the global marketplace. While the scope of Nortel's activities in the region encompasses enterprise, broadband, wireless and turnkey public carrier network solutions, the area of greatest activity involves wireless technology solutions.

- *Brazil*. Nortel established operations in Brazil in 1990, where it has significant shares of the country's data and transmission markets. Having recently won contracts to supply three out of four B-band licence winners, Nortel currently holds more than 20 percent of the Brazilian wireless telecommunications market.
- BCP and BSE, companies led by Bell South and Grupo Safra as well as Americel (a partnership of Bell Canada International, Telesystème and Citibank) chose Nortel as their exclusive supplier of network equipment and services.
- A cellular network infrastructure project will serve more than 500,000 subscribers in the state of Minas Gerais.
- *Mexico*. Nortel has been present in the country since 1989 when it started to sell small PBXs and key systems to businesses and other institutions. It has been an active participant in Mexico's rapidly expanding telecom infrastructure.
- In just 11 months, Nortel designed and built a complete telecommunications infrastructure for Avantel, an alternative carrier formed through a joint venture between MCI, one of the United States' largest long-distance operators, and Banamex-Accival, the largest commercial bank in Mexico.

- As the first major electronics manufacturer to eliminate ozone-depleting CFC-113 for its manufacturing operations worldwide, Nortel helped small- and medium-sized industries in Mexico become CFC-113 free by making its technology publicly available.
- *Colombia*. This is one of Nortel's fastest-growing markets in North America.
- Nortel will provide a complete telecommunications infrastructure, involving more than 750,000 lines, throughout the country.
- The company has captured more than 75 percent of the Colombian cellular market.
- *Chile*. Nortel will deploy a nationwide cable telephony network — the first in Latin America. This project will involve an expansion of service by more than 350,000 lines.
- *Bolivia*. A high-capacity fixed wireless network, featuring digital wireless technology, is being supplied here.
- *Venezuela*. Nortel has installed one of the largest ISDN networks in Latin America with Lagoven of Venezuela.
- *Peru*. Nortel has expanded its presence through the strong performance of its cellular and multimedia systems business.
- *Guyana*. Guyana Telephone & Telegraph has turned to Nortel for the deployment of a network with a total of 2,000 fixed wireless access lines.

In addition, those Central American countries using Nortel's digital switching systems in their networks include Honduras, Nicaragua, Panama, Guatemala, El Salvador, Costa Rica and Belize.

VI
Competing in Southeast Asia

Multinationals and Local Firms: The Best of Both Worlds

Terence Tsai

*Terence Tsai is professor of inter-
national business at the Richard
Ivey School of Business.*

With the rapid globalization of the business enterprise and the increasing dominance of Western management philosophy, Southeast Asian firms are being challenged by the need to conform. As international trade features more prominently in their business dealings, local Asian companies are engaging in a partial adaptation of Western management practices, yet are striving to retain their core management philosophy. Although Southeast Asian firms are accepting the concepts of greater decision-making transparency, institutionalized management codes, and lean management — common Western management philosophies — a full adaptation is not necessarily the best answer. Although the current financial crisis has exposed the structural and financial weakness of many conglomerates in the region, further necessitating the need to innovate their current ways of doing business, there are some advantages to the local firm that should be maintained.

Analysis of the merits of the multinational conglomerate (MNC) and the Southeast Asian enterprise, shows that size is undoubtedly a key differentiating factor. While the majority of Southeast Asian firms are small- to medium-scale, with corporate headquarters located in close proximity to their business activities, MNCs are much larger and often have their central decision-making centers based at head offices in the West. As a result, MNCs experience very little local cultural influence.

But there are advantages to be gained from both management styles. The main competitive attributes of the MNC management philosophy can be summarized in two categories — access to resources and consistency.

Access to Resources

As major MNCs rely upon a set of global standards to govern their management practices, the wealth of their international experience and greater numbers of management personnel often serve as conduits to a broader management approach. It also leads to a greater transferability of innovation, where an approach used in one geographic location, with certain modifications, can be transferred to and implemented in another location. The MNC's access to skilled international managers through vast global networks is also more expansive. The MNC's large scale and often abundant financial resources allow for the capability to absorb and operationalize new management concepts worldwide. But despite their grand scale, the MNCs are starting to place an increased emphasis on acting locally. Although affected more by time constraints, the MNCs' ability to diffuse management knowledge and simultaneously accumulate locally acquired knowledge forms an interesting positive feedback cycle that is not common to local firms.

Consistency

Because of their global management standards, the MNC experiences relatively little impact on overall operations from changeovers in personnel. Key investment projects often continue with minimal interruption, and the stakeholder can expect a constancy in the management performance level. However, local Asian enterprises, owing to their strong familial ties, often depend heavily on one key management figure to ensure the smooth management of the firm. If that manager leaves the firm, not only does this introduce turmoil throughout the company as other family members vie for the position, but overall operations are often greatly disturbed.

However, Southeast Asian firms, besides being family-based, are generally a more cohesive unit. This stems from their relatively small size and their focus on the regional market. Large corporations such as Goldstar and Kia in Korea, or Sony and Honda in Japan, are rare in Southeast Asia. But lacking the scale advantage does have its positive side — business transactions are easier to monitor and the diffusion of information within the corporate network is faster. Southeast Asian firms, too, are well embedded in the local societal matrix. As such, they have better linkages with the regional network. There are two key factors that characterize the managerial advantage of the local firm: speed and employee loyalty.

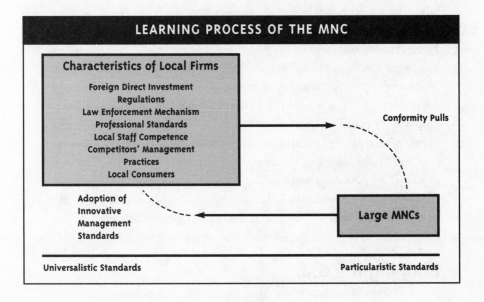

LEARNING PROCESS OF THE MNC

Characteristics of Local Firms

Foreign Direct Investment
Regulations
Law Enforcement Mechanism
Professional Standards
Local Staff Competence
Competitors' Management
Practices
Local Consumers

Conformity Pulls

Adoption of
Innovative
Management
Standards

Large MNCs

Universalistic Standards

Particularistic Standards

Speed

Southeast Asian firms are well adapted to respond quickly to changing market conditions. The market dynamic in Southeast Asia is one of the most vibrant in the world, necessitating a need for swift business actions. The small scale of the firms, to a certain degree, also implies that there is a smaller hierarchical structure within the organization. The standard codes of management, such as investment approval processes and employee grievance policies and procedures, are often nonexistent. As the firm is managed as a family unit, informal business proposals and oral approvals are common, enabling the firm to reach key strategic decisions within a shorter time frame.

Employee Loyalty

As the dominant management philosophy in the Southeast Asian firm revolves around family, managers serve the dual role of supervisor and parental figure. There is a generous level of profit-sharing, which would be considered quite high by Western standards. A typical year-end bonus at a Taiwanese enterprise, for example, totals three months' salary. In recent years, microelectronics firms in Taiwan, because of favorable trade conditions brought about by the devaluation of the New Taiwan dollar and subsequent record profit levels, have rewarded their employees with up to two years' salary and company stock ownership options. As the family structure is central to managing a local firm, the practice of looking after the well-being of each employee is considerably different from the Western style of management. Abuse of the system is rare — loyalty is paramount. Thailanders and South Koreans, for example, contributed their gold jewelry to save their countries from recent economic suffering. In Southeast Asian firms, strong employee loyalty reduces turnover levels and the costs associated with the hiring and training of new personnel.

Bridging the Gap

To be successful in Southeast Asia, foreign managers need to understand the fundamental cultural differences. The MNC that respects the local firm would benefit greatly from their expertise. One step involves hiring an intermediary who is well versed in local management philosophy as well as in the more subtle business and cultural practices of the region. Other steps involve establishing a direct reporting relationship between head office and selected local personnel, and making provisions to take advantage of local management expertise by facilitating timely approvals of strategic investment projects. Further, the local MNC subsidiaries should be encouraged to engage in various community projects to achieve a healthy blend of corporate and local culture. An effort to retain local employees and formulate a remuneration scheme based on local practice would also benefit the MNC. In turn, local firms should consider ways in which they could institutionalize their essential management practices, including a greater scrutiny of business decisions, without sacrificing the informal family atmosphere. This step is of great importance as one of the key inducing factors of the Asian financial crisis was the inability to blend the two management styles. The favor shown toward family, for instance, often led to poor business decisions that were detrimental not only to the survival of the firm, but also to the financial well-being of the region.

Southeast Asia holds many wealth-creating business opportunities and remains a land of adventure for Canadian firms. But beyond investment in financial capital should be a comparable investment in social capital. A better understanding of the regional environment and business practices will afford all players the opportunity to experience the rewards of bringing together the best of both worlds.

A Look at the Dynamics of Asian Business and Culture

John H. Eggers

John H. Eggers is a professor at the Institute for Entrepreneurship, Innovation and Growth at the Richard Ivey School of Business.

Even with the recent economic slowdown throughout the Asian region, Asia is still the most vibrant market in the world. The potential for growth is enormous — China in particular is not only the fastest-growing market, it will soon be the world's largest. With a population of more than one billion, and the financial and shipping center of Hong Kong as its hub, China is a critical region for foreign business managers doing business internationally. According to a recent study conducted by Ernst & Young, the region's real GDP, excluding Japan, will grow by a remarkable 7.3 percent per year over the next decade.

For any player in the world economy, doing business in the Far East should be part of the strategic plan of any growth-oriented organization. Having lived and worked in Asia for the past six years, I have some observations that might be useful for foreign managers looking to maximize their success and minimize the risks of doing business in such a vibrant region.

Asia contains a vast multitude of cultures, value systems and languages within its nations. Any marketing or business plan must address the needs and cultural diversity of each individual country. Plans that generalize across the region without taking local differences into account will achieve little success.

In the well-established centers of Singapore, Hong Kong, Taipei, and Seoul — favorite headquarter sites for several Western companies — locals have seen many companies come and go. Although a company may be successful in its home market, this does not ensure success in Asia. It is important to remember that business is conducted through relationships much more so than it is in Western countries. It takes years to form and develop the relationships a company needs, and to build the trust necessary to do business. Korea, for example, is one region where establishing business connections can be an especially long process.

Social positioning and presentation are also critical, including graduating from a reputable university. Alumni tend to stay in touch even decades after they have left school. And attending what is viewed as a lesser school can impede or eliminate access to critical decision-makers. Further, if a company is not financially committed for the long haul, then managers may want to wait until they are in the position to distribute directly into these markets.

Finding a reputable, established company to be a distributor or local partner is a good place to start, as is becoming known as a credible source with local connections. If managers choose to establish their own local organization, it is critical to involve management and employees from the local area. There are a number of highly qualified individuals who can offer critical language skills, a key understanding of doing business locally, and help a company establish goodwill throughout the business region. Although these local personnel can be costly and turnover rates are high — a direct result of a low unemployment level and a minimum of available and well-trained business graduates — it is worth the added investment.

It is also important to be aware of some key cultural and business nuances that are common throughout Asia. Business in Asia is conducted courteously and respectfully, and at a slower pace — foreign managers who do not act in a polite manner will not be well received. Second, it is common to discuss at length and in great detail the issues surrounding the company's products or services. Although managers begin to establish their credibility at these initial meetings, and even after much time and effort has passed, negotiations can still go either way. It is important not to misinterpret multiple meetings with a potential client as a commitment to buy.

Third, it is common practice to provide gifts to company or government representatives in order to bring proposals to a close or to obtain critical business documents or permits. This is especially true in China (not Hong Kong), Indonesia, Korea and the Philippines. Foreign managers should avoid misinterpreting this traditional business practice — it is an important custom that shows respect. Since this practice may be viewed as unethical and may even be considered illegal for Western-based companies, the use of a local distributor to act as the interface between the local client and home office can remove any potential liability.

Fourth, ensure that all immigration and import/export paperwork is in good order. A local lawyer can help foreign managers ensure that they have the documentation required. In some countries, for example, the penalty for an expired visa is 30 days in the local jail.

Finally, copyright and patent protection laws differ greatly in Asia from those in the West, and due diligence is required to minimize damage to a foreign company's service or brand. Although great strides are being made to upgrade these laws, managers should ensure their complete protection. Intel, for example, has experienced major problems with their 100 Hz Pentium chips being "tweaked" and resold at a higher price. Companies can receive sound advice and counsel from local legal representatives. Further, managers may wish to first establish their markets in regions such as Hong Kong or Singapore where such practices are uncommon.

In some areas counterfeit funds are also a significant problem. Reproductions of the U.S. $100 bill were so accurate even the local banks could not detect them. It is estimated that millions, perhaps even a billion, of these bills are still in circulation and may never be detected. The United States modifed and reissued the U.S. $100 bill to eliminate the widespread fear that U.S. currency would be destabilized in Asia.

Undoubtedly, Asia is one of the world's most exciting places to do business and opportunity continues to abound. With some basic precautions and an understanding and appreciation of local traditions and customs, a foreign organization may find a ripe market for their product or service. If a company is to be a global player at all in the coming decade, it will need to be a player in Asia.

Some Do's and Don'ts on Managing in Asia

Joseph J. DiStefano

Joseph J. DiStefano is a professor of organizational behavior at the Richard Ivey School of Business. He is the Shirley Chan Memorial Professor of International Business and the executive director of Ivey's executive MBA program based in Hong Kong.

The current volatility of Asian financial markets, the ever-changing legal and regulatory conditions of doing business in the region, and the continuing competitive pressures of managing people across complex and often subtle cultural diversities of Asian countries continue to be top priorities for senior executives doing business there. Although the financial shocks of the past few months and the resultant downsizing may moderate the difficulty of recruiting and keeping well-trained staff in many parts of Asia, the demand for effective managers in the region remains high. As such, dealing effectively with multicultural realities in Asia remains of key importance.

Principles for Cross-Cultural Effectiveness

The key factors to cross-cultural effectiveness identified in the study I conducted more than 25 years ago are still relevant. Although emphasis within each theme has shifted slightly, the following principles remain as useful guidelines for executives doing business in Asia.

1. Deciding to Operate in Asia

- *Don't underestimate people problems.* Very recently a Canadian executive called for advice on a major investment opportunity in a food processing facility in the Sichuan province of China. All of his questions focused on market conditions and regulatory, legal and financial issues. Having just visited similar operations in the same city, I emphasized to this individual the importance of considering human resources issues as well. Finding skilled hourly employees remains a key challenge to effectively conducting business in many parts of the Asia-Pacific.
- *Do include cultural issues in estimating costs and developing plans.* Assumptions about human behavior, if based on company success in North America, are likely to be wrong when applied to an Asian context. Many multinationals have made this mistake and have experienced high levels of turnover. Further, if expectations of high individual initiative and quality customer service are to be met, then selection, training and development costs are also likely to be high. While the work ethic among employees in Hong Kong and in many other parts of the region is exceptional, the differences in ways of managing individuals require foreign managers to adapt to Asian ways of doing business. Following are some examples of what adaptations are needed and how to implement them.

2. Operational Issues

- *Don't exclude yourself as part of the problem.* It is human tendency to credit yourself with successes and blame others when problems arise. In cross-cultural situations, the likelihood of problems increases, as does the tendency to blame others. Looking at the part your behavior plays in any problem is a useful guide to use in any situation; and it is even more useful when facing cultural differences. Further, don't hesitate to apologize for any errors you may make. While in many parts of Asia such a gesture is likely to be met with protests that there is no problem, you build goodwill by making the attempt.

- *Do try to learn and adapt.* In recent years managerial information about doing business in specific countries has become readily available in books, "culturgrams" (summaries of appropriate behavior by country) and videos. But even with such guidelines, it is useful to have a broader framework to make sense of your own experience. Further, with the high numbers of expatriate managers responsible for their company's Asian division and working in multicultural teams, having a comprehensive conceptual scheme is important. Martha Maznevski and I developed a proven model for achieving high performance that has been widely used throughout Asia, North America and Europe. The "MCI" model is based on three key features. The first — *Map* — is about mapping or learning about the key aspects of the cultural differences at play, including the understanding of your own culture and how it affects your work behavior. The second component — *Communication* — involves taking stock of what motivates you and suppressing the tendency to blame others. Using your cultural maps, you can learn to better understand the other person's frame of reference and to develop common modes of communicating. As competence in intercultural communication is gained, then the next step — *Integration* — follows. This consists of focusing on the other person's involvement, resolving conflicts and building on each other's ideas. These are effective behaviors to integrating cultural differences and achieving higher performance.

3. Expatriate Selection

- *Don't rely solely on technical competence.* Twenty-five years ago a major study by Edward Miller revealed that although many companies understood that "soft skills" were important in selecting expatriate employees, they continued to rely primarily on technical expertise when choosing people for overseas assignments. Many years later another major survey, conducted by Rosalie Tung, showed that this practice has not changed. Indeed, success in foreign assignments depends on more than functional expertise alone; avoid at all costs using it as a sole selection criterion. With educational standards being raised for Asian managers and more being educated outside their own countries, narrow technical competence in expatriates is less important than ever.

- *Do selection in stages and broaden criteria.* Before selecting an expatriate, first gather information about the requirements of the position beyond the job itself. Then, address the issues of language, local housing and educational facilities and the cultural and economic conditions of the employment area. In developing selection criteria, keep in mind that overseas effectiveness, according to extensive research by scholars around the world, depends as much on adaptation and interactional skills as it does on technical expertise. Finally, research also shows that contrary to conventional wisdom, women expatriates in Asia and elsewhere have excellent success rates. So include them in your pool of candidates.

4. Training and Development

- *Don't omit families.* Although multinationals sending expatriates and inpatriates to and from Asia are doing a better job than ever of providing language and culture training, many companies continue to neglect the importance of spouse and family to the manager's relocation. Although the incoming manager is provided these necessary tools to facilitate their adjustment, the spouse is not considered as needing the same support. The more advance information and training you can provide, the more likely the family's adjustment will be successful. In light of the extraordinary costs of employee turnover due to family problems, investment in training prior to departure is wise from both a financial and human resources perspective.

- *Do include cross-cultural training.* Among the key elements in training for Asian cultures is sensitivity to relationships. The predominance of individualism and the high task orientation of the North American work ethic can make many expatriates from Canada and the United States unaware of the subtleties of relationships. It is important to remember that: (a) relationships are important in themselves; and (b) without establishing a network of trusting relationships with key players, getting things done will be slower and more difficult. And remember that it takes time for effective relationships to be built. Our own research has demonstrated that even two days of training based on the MCI model can help managers be more effective. As one CEO of a large U.S. imaging company said, "The most important thing to know about working in other cultures is what you don't know." Training is the key to awareness.

5. Culture Shock

- *Don't neglect the warning signs.* No matter how carefully personnel have been selected and trained, some degree of culture shock is inevitable, even for experienced internationalists. Irritability, lowered performance and withdrawal from daily activities are common indicators. Note, too, that culture shock is not only associated with entry into a new culture, but occurs with re-entry to one's home country. A successful Hong Kong executive returning after several years in Canada reported recently that she experienced people as rude and unfriendly, and that her friends said she "sounded like an alien." She later reported that it took more than two years to re-acclimatize: "You may speak the same language, but you think differently," she remarked.

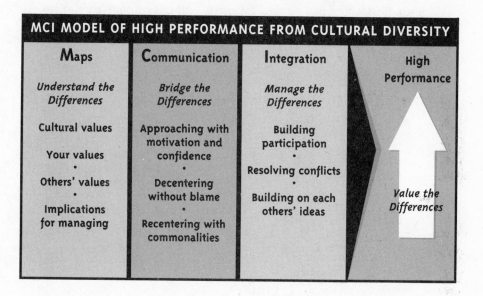

MCI MODEL OF HIGH PERFORMANCE FROM CULTURAL DIVERSITY

Maps	**Communication**	**Integration**	**High Performance**
Understand the Differences	*Bridge the Differences*	*Manage the Differences*	
Cultural values	Approaching with motivation and confidence	Building participation	
Your values	•	•	
•	Decentering without blame	Resolving conflicts	
Others' values	•	•	*Value the Differences*
•	Recentering with commonalities	Building on each others' ideas	
Implications for managing			

- *Do provide support during the transition.* Increasingly companies are providing expatriate support at their foreign sites. Local bicultural "coaches" are designated to assist managers through the adjustment period. They are responsible for maintaining links with expatriates, and assisting them with both the acclimatizing and the re-entry period of adjustment. The best practice, although rare, includes some cultural reorientation for returning families.

When the first version of these guidelines appeared in the 1970s, many people predicted that with cheaper and more effective international communication and transportation capabilities, the need to manage cultural differences would diminish. Despite the fact that global business is now a reality and that advances in computer and transmission technologies have eased international communications beyond expectation, cultural factors have maintained a significant impact on how work is done. The closing caution from that earlier study seems as appropriate now as it was then. Managers coming to Asia from other parts of the world would do well to heed the advice of Dostoevsky in *The Brothers Karamazov*: "Reforms, when the ground has not been prepared for them, especially if they are institutions copied from abroad, do nothing but mischief."

The Asian Crisis: What Are the New Risks?

David W. Conklin

David W. Conklin is a professor of international strategy at the Richard Ivey School of Business.

How can an investor make sense of the fallout from the Asian financial crisis? For some potential investors, the miracle of exceptionally rapid growth has ended, and a number are shifting their attention from Southeast Asia to other investment sites around the globe. Whether assessing what will happen with current Asian investments or considering future ones, it is necessary for investors to look at how the foreign exchange crisis has affected the financial and business sectors, and the overall economy of each Asian country.

The Asian foreign exchange crisis has dramatically altered the country risks and competitive advantage in Asia. Although strengthening the export sectors, the currency devaluations have severely damaged both the import sectors and businesses serving the domestic market. Indeed, U.S. and Canadian businesses that have sold products or components to

Asian customers have cause for concern. But the Asian crisis has not afflicted all countries equally — an analysis of each individual country is necessary to determine the severity of its effects.

In addition, the Asian crisis has impacted each business sector differently. The falling international value of Asian currencies is making exports from these countries cheaper in U.S. and Canadian dollars, strengthening the export sector. Consequently, a potential investor may see the situation as an opportunity to invest. But at the same time, falling international values of Asian currencies are making imports into these countries more expensive in their local currency, weakening the import sector. A potential investor in the import sector or in an Asian business that relies heavily on imports may consider this situation as a long-run country risk. For certain countries like Indonesia and Malaysia, for example, the extension of the foreign exchange crisis to the financial sector, and indeed to the economy overall, threatens to reduce domestic demand at both the corporate and consumer levels.

Another important issue to consider is whether the International Monetary Fund (IMF) bailout efforts will succeed. To address the currency issue, it is first necessary to examine the link between the foreign exchange crisis that each country faces and the banking system of that country. It has become apparent that many banks in several regions are insolvent, and this reality has turned the foreign exchange crisis into a financial one. As some banks close and others call in their loans to maintain solvency, many businesses are being hurt and the overall economy is being dragged down.

Political Risks

In many Asian countries bank loans were granted as favors to political leadership, often without due diligence. The foreign exchange crisis has revealed that a very high percentage of loans are non-performing. As a result, many banks are going under, and financial systems are in disarray. A democratic political system generally does not experience the spread of a foreign exchange crisis to its financial sector and its general economy as politicians are held accountable by the public. Both the opposition and the media bring to the public's attention any bank loans given for political affiliation. For some Asian countries this has not been the case. Unless there is a basic shift in the political paradigm, the financial sector disaster may occur again — economic reform requires political reform.

The Asian crisis may become worse if the difficult situation faced by China's banks surfaces. Political loans by Chinese banks to now-suffering state-owned enterprises have created the risk of financial collapse. The development of alternative financial instruments could result in a reduction in deposits at domestic Chinese banks. Hence, the liberalization of the Chinese financial sector, combined with the growth of the stock exchange and the expansion of foreign banks, may lead to the collapse of the country's domestic financial sector. Here, a change in the political system with a new financial account-ability of state-owned enterprises is necessary before a sound financial system can emerge.

The IMF Bailout

The IMF has offered most Asian countries rescue packages consisting of foreign currency to support each country's international exchange rate. Although these efforts have often been successful in other areas of the world, the effect of the crisis on the Asian economy is different. The problem runs very deep — for some countries the crisis extends to the financial sector and their economy as a whole. The IMF rescue packages may stabilize foreign exchange rates in the short term, but they will not eliminate the financial crisis, the damage to many businesses, nor the risk of economic recession.

Some argue that the Asian economy will instead be hurt by the IMF's efforts. Since the IMF insists upon a considerable tightening of monetary and fiscal policy as a condition for the loans, the effects of these measures could worsen the financial crisis and heighten the potential of an economic recession. As foreign exchange volatility is reduced, the country risk for potential investors increases. The Indonesian currency board debate illustrates this dilemma. Some argued that the Indonesian rupiah should be pegged at a certain fixed exchange rate to the U.S. dollar. An independent currency board would supervise the money supply with the sole objective of maintaining this fixed rate. The money supply would be backed by reserves of dollars, and expanded only in accordance with the rate of foreign currency inflows. Such a commitment might at times require extremely high interest rates to attract the capital inflows that would support the fixed rate. Even the IMF has argued that a currency board approach could create economic devastation in a future exchange crisis, and that some future exchange rate flexibility may be necessary.

Further, the Asian crisis has created a new risk of heightened foreign exchange volatility for some countries. Exchange rates were maintained at unrealistically high levels as a result of considerable inflows of foreign capital. Now, the optimism of the foreign investor has been replaced by caution. Capital flows will now be much more sensitive to changes in each country's financial system and general economic conditions than they have been in the past. This surge in capital flows activity may translate into increased volatility of foreign exchange rates for some countries.

For financial institutions everywhere, an ongoing challenge is that the time profile of liabilities is not the same as that of assets. Banks borrow short-term from depositors and lend long-term. This exposes the banks to the risk that fixed assets may fall quickly in price and that depositors may make sudden withdrawals. Further to the non-performing loan problem, Asian banks are confronted with dramatic reductions in land and stock prices. Bank loans made on the security of real estate and stocks suddenly are at a major risk of default, further exacerbating the effects of the financial crisis overall.

The insurance sector also faces problems caused by the difference in time profile of assets and liabilities. In Japan, insurance companies have based their premium schedules on expectations that they would be able to earn reasonable rates of return. However, over the past decade, Japanese interest rates have been far below the levels necessary to earn expected returns. Consequently, the Japanese insurance sector faces new solvency risks — a problem that may also add to the Asian financial crisis.

The Central Bank Dilemma

During the recent fall of the Canadian dollar, many people maintained that Canada's central bank should have raised interest rates to prevent it from slipping below US$.70. But the Bank of Canada faced the dilemma that by increasing domestic interest rates they could in turn hurt the Canadian unemployment level. And the Asian central banks face this same dilemma. Should they raise interest rates in order to attract capital inflows and stabilize their currency? If so, the risks of a general recession increase. There is a sharp contrast between the interests of Asian central banks and those of the IMF. While the IMF places priority on the stabilization of the exchange rate, central banks will sometimes have to sacrifice foreign exchange stability in order to support jobs and their domestic economy.

Should Depositors Be Protected?

The Canada Deposit Insurance Corporation provides a guarantee to depositors in case of the insolvency of the institution in which they have put their money. This guarantee is based upon the gradual accumulation of insurance funds in which all banks participate by paying a small premium. Asian financial systems do not have this kind of deposit insurance protection. Now, Asian political leaders face the difficult question of whether they should use public funds to reimburse depositors in insolvent banks. Should public funds also be used to assist the businesses whose domestic bank loans or foreign borrowings have placed them in jeopardy in the new business environment? If the governments do not take a rescue position, then the financial crisis may have a greater negative impact on the economy as a whole.

What Does the Future Hold?

Instead of viewing Southeast Asia as a group of "tigers" that have been involved in an economic miracle and subsequent downfall, it is now necessary to analyze carefully the situation that each individual country faces. Taiwan, South Korea, and the Philippines, for example, are likely to achieve a new competitive advantage for many of the businesses currently located there. Some countries, such as Singapore, Taiwan and Hong Kong, do not have a serious bank insolvency problem, and for them, the Asian crisis may pass relatively quickly and without any terribly serious impact on their economies.

For Canadians who are searching for Asian suppliers and customers, as well as Canadians who are evaluating investment opportunities, the analysis of country risks has attained a new importance. Asian growth funds will have to differentiate more carefully among countries and business sectors. Although the Asian crisis may have changed the way the game is played, the game is still on.

Opening the Door to a New World

Henry Cheng

Dr. Henry Cheng is managing director of New World Development and a graduate of Ivey's MBA program. A businessman who has spent many years working in and with China, Dr. Cheng was instrumental in the establishment of Ivey's Asian Management Institute.

I am often asked what the secret is of successfully doing business in the People's Republic of China (PRC). Although there isn't any simple answer, the experience that New World Development Company (NWD) has gained through the growth of its business in China over the past 18 years may shed some valuable light on this complex question.

New World is now the single largest Hong Kong investor in China, with more than US$3.8 billion invested in the region. We are involved in a tremendously diverse range of long-term ventures, including a total of US$1.5 billion invested in infrastructure projects, such as highways, bridges, cargo-handling facilities, cement plants and power stations. We have major investments in government-subsidized low-cost housing, industrial parks, commercial developments and city core redevelopment projects, where we demolish and rebuild entire districts within China's older city centres. More recently, we have become partners with the Chinese government in transforming some of the best and most promising of its 300,000 state-owned enterprises into viable businesses.

How did New World's journey begin and what lessons have we learned along the way?

A Partner in Meeting China's Needs

New World became one of the first outside investors in China in 1980, shortly after economic reforms began in 1978. My father, Dr. Cheng Yu-tung, arranged the first-ever foreign joint venture hotel in China. The Guangzhou China Hotel was developed by a consortium of Hong Kong investors. New World was an investor and principal manager of this project.

From the beginning we have been true partners in helping the Chinese government to modernize its economy and make the challenging, long-term transition from a command- to a market-based economy. The economic transformation has been remarkable, with China emerging as one of the world's fastest-growing economies. Since 1978, GDP has tripled, per capita incomes have more than quadrupled, growth has been in double-digit figures for much of the past decade, and inflation has been brought under control. Since 1990, almost 300 foreign companies have invested more than US$10 million. Prior to 1990, only 25 companies had investments of US$10 million in China.

New World has participated in and benefitted greatly from this economic growth. But it hasn't been easy and there have been many obstacles along the way. The key to our success is that we've made it our business to fully understand what China's needs are. We focus our efforts on helping both the national and local city governments meet their most critical goals and priorities.

Since the early 1980s, New World has helped China to implement such basic but essential services as roads, power stations, bridges and low-cost urban housing. We have invested substantial capital in these ventures, and provided the management and technical expertise required to carry out and complete major infrastructure and housing projects in the cities of Beijing, Tianjin, Guangzhou and Wuhan, as well as several smaller cities.

Such endeavors often carry great value and deep meaning for local communities because of the considerable impact they have on improving the daily lives and future prospects of the millions of people in each region. For example, we invested more than US$100 million to build three toll bridges across the Yangzi and Han rivers in the inland port city of Wuhan, a city that was not initially part of China's economic boom. "Building these new bridges has been the goal and aspiration of Wuhan people for 40 years," explained Hu Zhao Zhou, the vice-chairman of Wuhan's City Council, to *Asia, Inc.* magazine. "We couldn't build any bridges before. We were short of money. The Cheng family has helped Wuhan very, very much. We were at a great hour of need."

We were there for Wuhan when they needed us and China has reciprocated. NWD has received a generous "in perpetuity" owner-ship position of almost 49 percent of the Wuhan bridges, whereas many other infrastructure investments have 25-year to 30-year expi-ration dates. The Wuhan bridges have been the gateway to a much broader development and revitalization of the region. We now have a total of US$450 million invested in Wuhan projects, including low-cost housing, toll roads, industrial parks and high-end commercial and office space.

Demonstrating Commitment

We know the importance of timing in meeting China's needs: New World has always had a strong belief in the future success of China. We have demonstrated our unwavering commitment to China's future through periods of political and economic uncertainty by continuing to make major investments, particularly when China needs them most. For example, just two days after the death of Comrade Deng Xiaoping, we stood by our commitment to China by purchasing 9.9 percent of Beijing Data Power Generation Co. for US$160 million, despite the political ramifications that had impacted the nation.

The Chinese government recognizes and appreciates that we are willing to back up our words with concrete actions. This has earned us their trust and respect, and given us the all-important credibility that outside investors must have to work successfully with Chinese joint venture partners at both the national and local levels. In turn, we've found that if we satisfy China's needs, at the same time we satisfy our needs and those of our shareholders.

When faced with financial obstacles in moving forward, we did not retreat, but looked for alternative solutions. In 1993, when China was facing double-digit inflation, New World reached an impasse in its infrastructure operations, and senior management was not eager to increase the parent company's debt load. We needed investors in the world community to come on board and support our long-term China strategy. This ultimately led to the formation in 1995 of New World Infrastructure, which has raised hundreds of millions of dollars for new projects and has since rewarded investors handsomely.

Risks and Rewards

Although we invest money in China, that does not mean we are insensitive to risk. When investing in an infrastructure project, we expect a payback period of money invested of roughly seven to eight years. Our strategy is clear: we want a diversified portfolio of projects in growth regions that can not only provide recurrent cash flows, but are complemented with demonstrated management expertise. This has been accomplished to date, with infrastructure projects earning annual returns in excess of 30 percent.

Solutions to Housing Needs

With a population of more than one billion — one-quarter of the world's population — China considers adequate and affordable housing for its people to be a major concern. New World has been proactive in providing viable solutions that meet China's most pressing social needs. As such, we raised more than US$800 million for low-cost housing and urban renewal projects through direct investment funds and syndicated loans from foreign banks and private investors.

In exchange for building homes, New World secures large blocks of land for commercial development as part of an urban renewal program we refer to as City Core Redevelopment. By forming partnerships with the government, we receive timely approvals of work schedules and licences. More interesting for shareholders is that we can lock in land premiums at deferred low prices, allowing for minimal carrying costs and upfront cash outlays. We have secured options on large parcels of land in prime locations, and presently have a land bank of more than 200 million square feet — bigger than all of Hong Kong. Massive redevelopment projects are going full speed ahead in Beijing, Tianjin, Shanghai, Guangzhou and Wuhan.

Commercializing State-Owned Enterprises

China's next goal is to revamp the best of its state-owned enterprises and upgrade them into viable commercial businesses. In two decades China has become a major global trading nation. This latest initiative is a critical next step in its evolution toward a market-based economy. Although a considerable challenge, this objective offers many attractive opportunities for discerning foreign investors.

Further, New World has set aside a fund of US$350 million, and plans to raise more capital to invest in the most promising enterprises that meet our business criteria. We don't claim or intend to be knowledgeable in all areas, and we are seeking foreign investors as strategic partners who could contribute technology and capital toward establishing joint ventures with us and local Chinese partners. For instance, in early 1998 we entered into a contract with a Canadian consumer packaging company to build two bottling plants in the region. Together, we bring capital, management expertise, excellent connections with the Chinese government, and our experience doing business in China to the venture. We are also targeting enterprises of the future in fields such as biotechnology, fiber optics, and information technology to take China into the 21st century.

Management Shortfall

A continuing challenge for outside investors considering doing business in China is the shortage of people with business and management skills. Foreign companies operating here are desperately short of trained managers who can act as a bridge between local workers and management and foreign investors. This management shortfall is most often met with expatriate managers. Our approach has been to bring in outside management in the early stages of a project and then develop the local talent. We are investing in the training of local managers so they can, in turn, train others. Although we often send local business people and government officials for instruction overseas, there continues to be an overwhelming need to develop the next generation of China's senior business managers.

The risks that New World has undertaken by expanding its business in China are paying important dividends today as Southeast Asia goes through a period of economic uncertainty. We are a cash-rich company and our diversification into a broad range of profitable projects in China, beyond our core development business, gives us added strength to weather economic storms.

Looking ahead, we will continue on our path as a partner helping China in its ongoing quest to become the world's largest economy in the 21st century. We are totally committed to helping China satisfy the basic needs of its people for food, housing, clothing and transportation, and will continue to diversify and grow our business in these key areas. We want to make New World Development part of the everyday life of all Chinese citizens.

Lessons Learned

There are many important factors to doing business successfully in China. You need to have a strong belief in the future success of the region and back up that belief with a steadfast commitment to carry you through periods of political and economic uncertainty. The key is to be patient and persevere.

There is a shortage of Western-style management skills in China and, as such, you should be prepared to provide the management capability and training required to accomplish your objectives.

It is also important to have a long-term view toward building healthy business relationships. You need to speak the same language — both literally and culturally. Foreign managers need to recognize that there are huge differences in how they and their Chinese counterparts conduct business. In China, becoming friends with prospective partners is a prerequisite to doing business with them. If you earn that friendship and demonstrate it in times of need, your government and business partners will stand by you.

It is not possible to succeed on your own in China. You have to find partners you can trust, appropriate joint venture partners, and the ability to provide "one-stop shopping" solutions to local governments. A key consideration is that the only true joint venture partner, when it comes to investing in China, is the PRC government. Above all, you have to be aware of China's needs and how you can meet them. That is the foundation on which you can build a mutually beneficial partnership. And once you've achieved this, you hold the key that can open the door to success.

China: The Hunter and the Hunted

Chen Xiaoyue

Professor Chen Xiaoyue is a professor of finance and associate dean of the School of Economics and Management at Tsinghua University and a visiting professor at the Richard Ivey School of Business.

Everything in the jungle looks gray at the break of dawn, much like the horizon faced by foreign investors looking to do business in China. You need somebody to help you navigate before you can learn enough to make it through on your own. It is a long march to reach your hunting place and if you find that the hunting is not as attractive as you expected, the path behind you is also long. Although the chase may be exciting, it is important to remain cautious and keep your eyes and ears open.

There is much material available on China — its market and industry, culture and people, systems and government, tradition and reform, natural and human resources, *guanxi* (connections) and corruption, to name a few. Each of these topics takes hundreds of pages to cover. But what has recently attracted most attention is the downsizing of China's government and the restructuring of its state-owned enterprises (SOEs).

The restructuring of SOEs has been the most difficult part of China's reform. After more than a decade of debate and many efforts to navigate the difficulty surrounding SOE restructuring, those who advocate a smaller and more efficient state-owned sector have emerged. But this reform will be a slow and laborious process. If the restructuring is successful, China may regain the momentum that has been recently diminishing from slower productivity improvement in state-owned and private sectors, and the swelling of government bodies. As a result, foreign investors may see better transparency of the system — less red tape, improved government efficiency and equal treatment of all enterprises. But in this process of transition, the environment may experience for a brief period — possibly two to three years — a much higher unemployment rate and increased social instability.

For a long time, the Chinese have recognized the necessity of downsizing and restructuring SOEs and the government. When the wolf does come, however, most people will have difficulty facing its bite. It is hard to imagine that a number of people equivalent to the entire Canadian population may be laid off in only two years. To absorb this wave of unemployment, many provisions must be made, including the development of a sound social security system that provides insurance and other social services; a high GDP growth rate that can generate millions of new jobs each year (a minimum of 6 to 8 percent); low inflation to curb social instability (which continues to be the government's first priority); and good performance in exports to create jobs and stimulate foreign exchange. In addition, it will be necessary to hold a stable exchange rate of Chinese renminbi (RMB) against the U.S. dollar to enhance foreign investor confidence.

Investors provide much-needed foreign capital and introduce advanced technology and management resources to the region. Whether these conditions can be met in the next year or in the near future is doubtful. However, the "soft landing" which took place two years ago brought about a very favorable environment that had achieved almost all of these conditions, demonstrating a much-improved control capability of the Chinese government over its economy.

The Asian Crisis

At first glance, and according to key economic indicators, the Asian financial crisis has had a very limited impact on China's economy. The growth rate remains at 9 percent; there is a 0.8 rate of inflation; the RMB is holding against the U.S. dollar; and a high export surplus and capital inflows into China continue. Over the long term, however, the effects of the crisis will be profound, especially in relation to the reorganization of China's economy. The burning question is how to reorganize — which model should China follow? Adopting a model based on Korean *chaebol* (conglomerates), for example, was one option considered by some Chinese officials as an adoptable pattern in forming new conglomerates for China's state-owned sector. But no clear model has yet been established, and it is likely that throughout the restructuring process, the Chinese government will continue to be cautious in its steps to integrate China's economy with the world's.

But China does not have time to wait for a more favorable international atmosphere. Premier Zhu Rongji has made his ideas very clear. Under his administration, China will restructure the government and the state-owned sector. To achieve this under a much cooler international investment environment, China will hold a moderate but tight money supply policy in order to maintain a stable RMB. But the cost of doing so — at a time when the growth rate is starting to decline — is a dangerously high unemployment rate. For most foreign investors, this is not a good scenario. However, there are some opportunities for portfolio investors in Chinese mergers and acquisitions. The newly restructured small- and medium-sized SOEs will be for sale in a few years. A reasonable assumption is that when thousands of these SOEs are made available to investors, they will hold a fairly low purchasing price.

Those who have waited to enter into a certain Chinese industry will find that this is not only the best approach, but the timing is right. Since most multinational enterprises (MNEs) can afford the high entry costs, a wholly owned subsidiary approach would be the prevailing choice. But keeping human resources expenses down, especially those associated with localizing senior and middle-level managers, is of top priority for many MNEs in China. Expatriate managers, although necessary in the startup phase, are very costly in the long run.

Making Connections

Establishing good guanxi is of crucial importance to doing business in China. They provide the necessary links to the Chinese culture and ways of doing business. It is important to make every effort to establish a good relationship with them. One tradition — drinking *maotai* — is one of most popular socializing activities for nurturing and developing guanxi. Having the right people on your team means that you must make the right connections and in the right way. Connecting with the wrong guanxi may result in trouble.

Protectionism and nationalism are also major concerns. To paraphrase James McGregor, vice-president and chief representative of Dow Jones in China, "China should say 'yes' to the world, but the question should be whether foreign investors would say 'no' to China." Or, to borrow a popular North American phrase, China appears to be both the hunter and the hunted.

VII
Power Play: The Role of the Board of Directors

Effective Boards Create Winning Strategies

Lawrence G. Tapp

Lawrence G. Tapp is Dean of the Richard Ivey School of Business.

Corporate governance is a hot topic today. Companies with strong, active and independent boards of directors have a powerful competitive advantage. However, even with strong evidence to support this, there continues to be much foot-dragging in many executive offices.

Recently I had the pleasure of speaking to members of the Institute of Corporate Directors and the Planning Forum about the roles that the board and executive management play in strategy formulation. As someone who has sat on both sides of the table, I have seen the benefits of what is considered good corporate governance.

Let's face it — in the past, many boards played, at best, a nominal role in the development of corporate strategy. Relinquishing real power to senior management or major shareholders, they became glorified rubber stamps, except in times of crisis or serious underperformance. It has been said that some corporate boards are essentially social clubs —

with an exclusive and potentially influential membership, but with little to do.

That is changing, but perhaps not as rapidly as it should. If Canadian companies are going to flourish in the global marketplace, directors must work together with senior management to develop effective competitive strategies. On the one hand, companies can't afford to neglect this source of expertise and experience. On the other, directors must take more seriously their role in maintaining and increasing shareholder value. But for this to happen, the governance process must be redesigned.

It has been said that directors are highly overpaid for what they do, but highly underpaid for what they should be doing. So what should they be doing? The traditional roles have been to advise senior management, assess the effectiveness of management and select and evaluate the CEO. I think that today's boards must go further — they must become partners in crafting the mission, vision and strategic positioning of their organization. They must direct and supervise strategic management and oversee the planning and implementation of the major changes needed to improve corporate performance. They must also represent the shareholders — all shareholders — in the deliberations of the company, and maintain good relations with them.

That is a big job that requires a skilled and knowledgeable cadre. At the risk of talking myself out of a job as a director serving on numerous public and private boards, I say that companies must take a whole new approach to the selection of their directors. It's no longer a question of recruiting individuals who are congenial with the existing board or who are relatives of major shareholders. The new director must have greater business sophistication in terms of industry experience, general management expertise and the ability to think strategically.

Directors should be carefully selected on the basis of position descriptions that identify specific responsibilities and duties. They should also be regularly evaluated against those responsibilities and, if found wanting, be replaced. There simply is no room for below-par performance.

Companies should not be timid in selecting a diverse group of directors — diverse in terms of industry experience, gender, ethnic background and professional training. This will broaden and deepen the quality of advice available for senior management. Further, most directors should be independent of the company. As such, they will be able to bring new perspectives to the table and be free to question and probe.

The corollary of this is that corporate directors and senior management must be prepared for dissent and disagreement. Strong, able directors will not see eye to eye with management or each other on every issue. Nor should they. Lively discussions and opposing viewpoints are the pulse of an effective board — a sign of life.

To recruit the right calibre of directors, companies must provide a substantially higher compensation scheme that is linked to short- and long-term corporate performance. With greater rewards, they can also expect more time and commitment from their directors.

The "garbage in, garbage out" rule applies to boards as much as it does to computer technology. To play a valuable role in the development of corporate strategy directors must be provided with good information. A well-organized orientation program for new directors is a valuable way to introduce them to the company, its industry and the major competitive issues it faces. Ongoing education and development for directors should also be available and encouraged. Information must flow to the directors on a regular and consistent basis, just as it does to other members of the senior management team.

Leadership is the key to forging an effective board. The chair plays a decisive role, creating the culture and setting the tone. A chair who avoids disagreement at all costs or is unquestioningly loyal to senior management will stifle other directors. One who encourages open discussion, demands professionalism and commitment from his or her directors, and works in a dynamic relationship with senior management adds tremendous value. The job of the chair is therefore critical. By recognizing and rewarding the substantial time demands and challenging job description, companies are better positioned to select and compensate their chair accordingly.

To be true partners in the development of corporate strategy, boards must be smaller and more agile than in the past. A board of more than 30 members is cumbersome and slow-moving. Many effective boards are considerably smaller.

The process of redesigning corporate governance is already underway in many Canadian companies. Researchers are continuing to identify the qualities that make a board effective and are both redefining and refining its role.

Together with many other top business schools, we at Ivey are doing our part to influence actions on corporate governance through teaching, executive development, management research and case-writing. Ultimately, however, it is the companies that will establish the rules of the game. They have nothing to lose and everything to gain. When senior managers work in partnership with strong, effective boards, the result is a well-thought-out corporate strategy — exactly what's needed to compete in today's highly competitive marketplace.

Making Boards Work

Donald H. Thain and David S. R. Leighton

*Donald H. Thain and David
S. R. Leighton are professors emer-
iti at the Richard Ivey School of
Business. This article is an excerpt
from their most recent book,*
Making Boards Work, *a
McGraw-Hill Ryerson publication.*

W hy do boards fail? This critical question, now
a defining issue in corporate governance,
remains largely unaddressed by shareholders, board
members and executives alike. In the absence of any
agreement on the answer, it is impossible to tackle
logically the ultimate issue: what should be done to
make boards more effective?

Clearly, not all boards fail. Some, to our first-hand
knowledge, work extremely well in fulfilling their
governance responsibilities. But such cases seldom get
reported. It is the spectacular failure — the aberration
— that draws public attention. The existence of well-
functioning boards proves the system can work as
intended. The challenge is to understand why some
boards fail and others succeed.

There are at least six major reasons why boards
fail. These reasons, which are all interrelated,

include failures of the following: leadership, power and legitimacy, job definition, competence, culture and board management.

1. Failures of Leadership

Quality of board leadership is undoubtedly the most critical of the key factors determining board success or failure.

As first among equals and the key link between the directors, shareholders and management, the chairman carries a heavy influence on the functioning of the board. As the primary planner and manager of the board's work, and leader of discussions at board and shareholder meetings, the chairman sets the tone, style, and pace and provides a model for all other directors.

Most of the problems of ineffective boards can be minimized or turned around if the board is led effectively. This means that the board, to be effective, requires leadership, and this leadership ordinarily comes from the chairman. In most North American boards, the chairman and chief executive officer are the same person. In such cases, the CEO is not only in charge of running the company, but is also responsible for running the board, to which he or she is theoretically accountable. It also means that the job of chairman is part-time and second in priority to the CEO task. When under pressure, the job of the chairman will almost always get short shrift.

There is an unspoken attitude that the board is a necessary evil; a burden on management whose influence is to be minimized. Board members are seen as part-time observers and outsiders, another layer of bureaucracy slowing things down.

The basic problem for many chairmen is that they lack the knowledge, attitudes, skills and experience to run an effective board. The job is seldom defined; qualifications are seldom thought through. Chairmen coming up the management ladder are usually appointed because they are good operators; they have strong functional expertise, the support of a strong mentor or good political skills; or they represent a powerful area in the organization — useful, but scarcely sufficient requirements for the job of chairman.

2. Failures of Power and Legitimacy

The authority, responsibility and influence of individual boards vary widely depending on the power they assume and the legitimacy of the source of that power.

If the board has the support and confidence of the firm's shareholders, and if the shareholders actively fulfill their rights and obligations as owners, the board can function as legally mandated. If not, its power tends to be taken over either by a major shareholder or by management, and its role is reduced to rubber-stamping decisions.

In many companies, chairmen who are CEOs concentrate power in their own hands and create a board of "spectators and cheerleaders" who are content to go along for the ride. Ordinary shareholders lack any voice, in part due to their own failure to exert their ownership rights. The institutions set up to give them a voice — the annual meeting, the proxy process, the nomination of directors — are merely charades whereby the board goes through the motions of consulting the owners, who are never challenged or held to account. The board is "elected" by the dominant CEO and chairman, thus breaking the essential accountability link with the ordinary shareholders. The result is power without accountability — a disaster waiting to happen.

3. Failures of Job Definition

Boards do not, cannot, run businesses in any active sense — they delegate this task to management. The best they can do is set or approve purpose and strategy, appoint officers, monitor their performance and hold them to account for results.

For whatever reason, meaningful job descriptions — standard practice at all other levels of the organization — are almost nonexistent at the board level, as is formal or systematic job training for directors.

Lack of agreement and precision on what boards are supposed to do makes it virtually impossible to measure whether any given board is effective and hence accountable.

4. Failures of Competence

The legal qualifications for directors or chairmen of corporations can sometimes set so low a hurdle that virtually anyone can be appointed a director, meaning that some directors are incompetent to perform the job of guiding a corporation. Coupled with an inadequate understanding of the job, it is not surprising that the criteria and selection processes for new directors are poorly designed.

Events of recent years have dramatically raised the bar for directors. Minimum requirements for being an effective director today are considerably higher than they were a decade ago. Knowledge of derivatives and other financial instruments was not an entry requirement for most directors serving today. The rapid growth of sophisticated information systems of the last 10 years has bypassed many directors. Environmental and social issues have transformed strategic thinking in many industries; and boards are being left behind because of changes in the technology of the business. Many directors are not up to the task.

Knowledge is power. In such circumstances, directors have little choice but to leave the most important strategic decisions in the hands of management, abdicating their most important responsibility.

5. Failures of Board Culture

Every board has a culture — the shared attitudes, values, experiences, norms and personal relationships that have built up over time and govern what directors say and do, and what subjects are taboo. In many boards, the culture is so deeply embedded that most directors are not aware of the possibility of doing things differently. This culture can be tremendously resistant to change.

Board cultures vary widely from what we have termed the "old code" — passive, accepting, deferring to the chairman and supporting management — to the "new code" — where participation is the norm, constructive dissent is encouraged and meetings are proactive. Culture largely determines whether the board will approach its tasks with a take-charge attitude or simply go along for the ride.

6. Failures of Board Management

The failure of many boards is due to bad management of the board itself. The size of a board, for example, can have a major impact on how effectively the individual director can work. Despite recent trends toward reducing board size, the boards of many public companies today are too large to be effective problem-solving groups.

When a board is too large, its flexibility is drastically reduced. Participation is limited. Meetings cannot be held on short notice or in response to crises without key members being absent. Agendas must be adhered to. Discussions must be limited. Time availability drives the board and its work. Formality and ritual become the norms.

The critical test of board administrations is management of the information function. Three common problems inhibit boards from doing their job: most data provided focus on past results rather than leading indicators; management controls the data provided; and too much data is sent out unedited.

Good board management releases the time of directors to focus on significant matters central to carrying out their responsibilities and improves the productivity of the board as a whole. Effective board management will not make up for other failings. But poor management not only hampers its effectiveness, it creates frustration and leads to underperformance or resignations from turned-off directors.

Key Success Factors for an Effective Board

Having reviewed the six principal reasons for board failure, here are six corresponding key success factors to building an effective board:

1. outstanding leadership;
2. unquestioned legitimacy and effective power;
3. enlightened definition of function, role and responsibilities;
4. a high level of competence;
5. a supportive, functional culture; and
6. efficient management of function, structure and process.

These six interrelated factors are the levers which must be controlled by those seeking to improve the quality of any board. Focusing effort on any one element will not produce the effect desired, although, if one of these factors is "first among equals," in our experience, it is leadership.

Corporate Financial Disclosure: Should Directors Monitor the Process?

Claude Lanfranconi and Darroch A. Robertson

Claude Lanfranconi and Darroch A. Robertson are professors of accounting at the Richard Ivey School of Business.

L egal responsibilities relating to financial statements and the disclosure of other financial information place a heavy burden on corporate directors. There have been frequent warnings of the hazards lurking behind the failure to meet certain mandated disclosure policies, and the danger of delays in releasing information. While this approach has received significant attention, directors are advised to take a more positive and proactive role in managing their corporate disclosure efforts. Boards need to develop a clear strategy in the disclosure of a company's financial information, as an aggressive effort to do so can improve a firm's competitive position in the marketplace.

Disclosure strategy involves senior management's methods of communicating financial information that are in accordance with the company's overall goals. A clear strategy in this area is vital, as decisions regarding the nature, amount and timing of information release directly affect the wealth of shareholders. This includes correcting misvaluations of company securities, increasing liquidity for the company's shares, changing the mix of shareholders or influencing the perceptions of government or the public. There is little doubt that Canadian banks as a group have developed and are implementing these approaches with their current advertising campaigns.

Value of Disclosure Strategy

What are the potential benefits associated with the development and implementation of a successful disclosure strategy? First, by employing such a strategy, management not only ensures that the company meets minimum statutory requirements, but reduces the probability of lawsuits against corporate directors. This makes it easier for organizations to attract quality directors. Directors who want to ensure quality leadership must ensure that there are systems in place that reduce liability exposure. The added benefit is that directors are protecting themselves while fulfilling their corporate governance obligations.

Another benefit of developing a proactive disclosure strategy is a potential reduction in the company's cost of capital. Individuals inside an organization, particularly senior management and directors, have access to a great deal of information about the expected future prospects of the organization. Strategic plans and preliminary market research, for example, are known to senior executives but are not necessarily available to the public. This creates an imbalance, known as "information asymmetry" in academic circles. Preliminary research suggests that companies can reduce their cost of capital by increasing their level of disclosure and consequently reducing the asymmetry. If management believes that their company is performing well and has good prospects, it is important to ensure that this information is sent, received and understood by company analysts.

Efforts to reduce information asymmetry are most beneficial in industries where company-specific information is not easily available from other sources or where the information is not easily verifiable.

For example, if the valuable assets of high-tech companies are not reflected in their financial statements, disclosure strategies to provide market participants with credible data relevant to the company's potential must be developed.

Empirical studies have shown that providing additional financial data can also reduce bid-ask spreads for a company's shares. Research measuring the extent of annual report disclosure of companies in the years leading up to a new issue of equity shows that companies increasing their disclosure prior to the year of issuance maintain this higher level once the equity has been raised.

The board should actively assess the company's financial accounting choices and its consequent reporting reputation, and determine if it is consistent with the image it wishes to project. Some of this information can be learned from determining how analysts perceive the company's corporate financial disclosure practices. Are the company's financial statements considered by the analyst community as reflecting conservative accounting policy choices, or are they viewed as more aggressive than competitors'? Does the company capitalize what other companies expense? Does it amortize slower or recognize revenue faster? At the very least it is important to know how the company is perceived if management intends to manage this process.

Developing a Positive Disclosure Strategy

1. Internal Monitoring and Actions

To communicate effectively outside the organization, management must implement an information system that addresses what is going on internally. The board of directors needs to be concerned about the existence of a reliable accounting information system that communicates relevant and timely data. These systems should be monitored by both internal and external auditors to ensure the directors know what is happening and are able to assess whether and how well the organization is operationalizing its current strategy. A strong internal audit group can prove invaluable in ensuring data integrity and enhancing disclosure strategy.

2. External Monitoring and Actions

In complying with statutory reporting procedures, a board should regularly review its current accounting policies decisions and their implementation. The company's accounting disclosure methods and estimates should permit outsiders to adequately monitor the operations and position of the company. There are a number of questions that should be asked: are there key measurements and disclosures that require special scrutiny? Have there been any recent changes in accounting standards? Has the implementation of these standards been adequately addressed? Are there any proposed accounting standards of interest? For example, recent accounting standards dealing with segmented reporting and the disclosure of financial instruments, or the proposed standard for postretirement benefits other than pensions, could have a significant impact on financial reporting. Management should discuss these potential changes and their consequences.

A company can also enhance its reporting position if it learns to work proactively with its auditor and treat these reporting partners as more than simply the cost of doing business. An important role for the outside director is to ensure that there is some separation between disclosure management and information manipulation. The directors, perhaps through the audit committee, need to create a climate where genuine give-and-take can occur. The board needs to be kept informed when there might be conflicts between management and its auditors. A first step is to consider the auditors' evaluation of the quality and quantity of the company's financial disclosure methods.

An example of the strategic nature of financial disclosure and accounting policy decisions is the recent merger discussions between the Bank of Montreal and Royal Bank, TD Bank and CIBC, and Nova Corporation and TransCanada PipeLines. In these situations the companies prefer to use "pooling of interest" vs. "purchase" accounting when producing consolidated financial statements. As purchase accounting requires that a combined operation reflects market values at the date of acquisition, and recognizes goodwill for any excess purchase price over the market values of identifiable assets and liabilities, it adds billions of dollars to the combined company's balance sheets and results in sharp increases of future expenses, such as the additional amortization of identifiable assets and goodwill. How the mergers are effected will have an impact on required accounting procedures. It is estimated that there may be approximately $11 billion of non-tax-deductible goodwill recorded if the Royal Bank/Bank of Montreal merger, for example, is treated as a "purchase." This would result in a more than $500 million deduction in annual income based on the 20-year amortization policy generally used by Canadian banks.

There is a considerable need for corporate boards to take a proactive approach in corporate financial disclosure. Corporate governance is not just about safekeeping and telling shareholders what has happened to the assets they have entrusted to the care of the board. To borrow a biblical analogy, it is not sufficient to bury the talents for safekeeping information only to be held responsible for reporting on their current status under pain of punishment. Corporate financial reporting can have a more positive benefit and should be managed in a way that can increase shareholder wealth. And research shows that making the effort can increase the potential for real return.

What Makes an Effective Board?

Brian Golden

Brian Golden is a professor of organizational behavior at the Richard Ivey School of Business.

As institutional investors continue to flex their growing financial muscle and take a more active role in monitoring publicly held companies, dramatic changes are beginning to occur in corporate boardrooms. In England, a committee headed by Sir Ronald Hampel of ICI, one of the world's largest chemical companies, recently recommended that the goal of a board of directors should encompass more than just passively monitoring managerial performance — it should more directly contribute to value creation in the firm. In another case, CalPERS, one of the largest pension funds in the United States, has issued its own checklist of best practices for a board of directors.

The image of the board most typically portrayed in the media is that of the "rubber stamp" — or, in other words, in no position to scrutinize the decisions and performance of managers. Historically, board membership was reserved to the elite in society, and thus, an invitation to sit on a firm's board was seen as a status symbol. Multiple board memberships for members of the elite were not uncommon, nor was it uncommon for a CEO of firm A to sit on firm B's board, while the CEO of firm B sat on firm A's board. The problem with this cozy relationship is clear when considering the primary responsibility of the board – to monitor the behaviors, decisions, and performance of the CEO, and ensure that the CEO is acting in the interests of the firm's shareholders. This responsibility grew out of securities law which, at the turn of the century, was a response to the growing division between those who owned the firm and those who managed it.

Recently there has been a broad-based shift in the makeup of the board. Underlying this move is the concern that managers may occasionally attempt to maximize their own well-being at the expense of shareholders. For example, management might fail to invest in research and development, with its long-term payouts, in order to maximize the short-term returns that influence the CEO's bonus.

Despite the movement to reconfigure the board, academics and industry leaders do not fully agree on what makes an "ideal" board. My ongoing research, with Professor Ed Zajac of Northwestern University in Illinois, involves looking at board member characteristics, the diversity of the board as a decision-making group, what board members actually do — or more importantly, what they often fail to do — and the power of the board in relation to the CEO. Following are three of the most important areas that affect board performance.

1. *Composition.* The relationship between a board's size and its ability to influence change diminishes after its size reaches 30 members. Boards that are too small place an undue burden on directors, so overloading directors that important responsibilities slip through the cracks. However, boards that are too large make for unwieldy group decision-making bodies. Also, since the board member's responsibility is often diffused in a large board, it's not uncommon to find members who don't make their fullest contribution. Boards also require some minimum level of diversity to have their greatest influence, such as involving members from a variety of professions and backgrounds, and representing different ages. However, too much diversity can lead to

dysfunction. Specifically, we found that while greater diversity can lead to the generation of novel and creative ideas, boards that are too diverse have difficulty agreeing on goals and making decisions.

There is a similar relationship with respect to how long members serve on a board. Although it is necessary for board members to sit on a board long enough to understand the organization, too long can lead to stagnancy — settling for the status quo. The regular infusion of new blood is critical to board effectiveness.

2. *Activity*. Whether a board is made up of today's business gurus, lawyers, community leaders or psychics is irrelevant if the board is not actively involved in monitoring the CEO's behaviors and performance, and working with the CEO to craft strategy. In fact, there is significant variation in how active boards are. At one extreme, many boards meet infrequently, rarely availing themselves of the information they need to monitor management's performance. At the other extreme are those boards which take the time and devote their energy to governing. For example, the most effective boards devote more time to the CEO evaluation process — a critical job if the board is to live up to its obligation of protecting the interests of shareholders.

3. *Power*. To say that boards are merely rubber stamps, as critics so often do, is to say that the board is weak. This kind of situation can arise when the CEO is both a board member and chair. Given that board membership is often considered a privilege, it is not surprising that board members appointed by the current CEO are more likely to be beholden to him or her. An illustration of this is seen in the case of Walt Disney's CEO Michael Eisner. Despite Disney's exceptional performance, critics had been concerned that the head of Disney's compensation committee was also Eisner's personal attorney — surely indicating a potential conflict of interest. Under pressure from institutional investors, the attorney was removed from that position.

In our research, we characterized boards as being more or less powerful (relative to the CEO) based on several indicators.

For example, boards are more powerful when the CEO does not nominate board members or when someone other than the CEO holds the position of chair.

Examining the power of the board relative to that of the CEO proved critical to our research. Virtually none of the correlations between board composition or activity was present for weak boards. However, these correlations were very strong for those boards characterized as influential. For a board to be effective, it matters little whether boards have the "right" members or whether the boards are active. What matters most is the presence of the three critical elements to designing the high-performing board: composition, activity and power. In the absence of any of these, boards will be merely rubber stamps, or worse yet , influential, but misguided. Only when all three are present can boards be effective partners.

The New Mandate for Shareholder Communications

Sarah Mavrinac and Henry Fiorillo

Sarah Mavrinac is a professor of accounting at the Richard Ivey School of Business. Henry Fiorillo is a management consultant in Toronto.

On any given day, the business media offer up stories of corporate failure. On some days, they focus on operating failures; on others, strategic failures — or they describe stories of outright fraud. Whatever the focus, the problem is inevitably made worse by the company's failure to communicate openly and honestly.

Consider, for example, *Business Week's* story on McDonald's that highlighted operating failures, marketing problems and disappointments in development. None of these problems is critical in itself, but collectively they are serious — especially given management's reluctance to communicate the logic of its strategy openly and honestly. Indeed, when operating problems are coupled with a communications shortfall, they become not just a management concern, but a governance issue.

Over the past 10 years, the Canadian investment community has witnessed a sea of change in investor expectations, and a new, rising interest in the concept and consequence of strategic investor relations (IR). The big institutional investors of today, the fund managers who watch over our pension funds, our mutual funds and the billions we have invested in RRSPs, are no longer content with the occasional press release or biannual conference call. They insist on serious, professional, and informed communications — on demand.

These investors know that IR isn't just another clever management concept. IR is an essential governance function that is fast becoming the purview of chief executive officers and corporate directors. Although IR has been a function of business for decades, it became the new corporate fashion in the spring of 1995 when the Toronto Stock Exchange established the Committee on Corporate Disclosure to review and evaluate corporate disclosure practices in Canada. The mandate of the committee was threefold: to review continuous disclosure by public corporations; to comment on the adequacy of such disclosure; and to "determine whether investors should be able to pursue private remedies if a company fails to comply with disclosure rules." Two years later, the committee published its final report and offered up arguments for a dramatic extension of investors' legal rights in the case of insufficient, inaccurate or misleading disclosures.

While ostensibly a study of disclosure practices in Canada, the report is essentially a statement of governance and investor rights. It is a statement of the criticality of the investor relations process and the responsibility of senior management to create a corporate culture that is responsive to the needs and interests of the global investment community. More significantly, it is a wakeup call for corporate directors to care about IR.

There are a host of reasons why all types of corporate managers should care. Over the past 10 years, a rich new set of studies has emerged that position the IR function as a strategic management issue with clear and measurable consequences for corporate performance. Differences in the quality of investor relations and in the timing of disclosures appear to be associated with decreases in volatility, a narrowing of bid-ask spreads, and an increase in market liquidity.

Studies conducted by researchers at the University of Michigan and Harvard Business School suggest that the quality of the IR function has a substantial impact on trading volumes and levels of institutional investment. Other studies suggest a relationship between IR and levels of research coverage and the accuracy of analysts' forecasts. Still others draw connections between the quality of investor relations and fundamental share values. For example, Sarah Mavrinac recently completed a study suggesting that millions of dollars of shareholder value can be created by undervalued firms simply by improving investors' perceptions of the quality of the firm's IR staff.

IR Strategy

IR is part public relations, part accounting, part journalism and a lot of finance. It's about talking to the markets — and it's important. Persuasive IR programs leverage three major communications vehicles: the company's accounting statements; its voluntary communication channels; and its capital structure and financing policies. But "strategic" investor relations is much bigger, involving a policy and set of communications procedures that function as an articulated part of the company's corporate and financing strategies. An IR strategy should express the company's plans for achieving a specific capital markets position.

To evaluate the effectiveness of an IR program, it is important to know whether it helps meet any of the company's significant goals. Is management happy with the coverage they get from Bay Street? Are they satisfied with their investor base? Do they know who their investors are? Are they satisfied with their share price? If the answer is "no" to any of these questions, it may be time to make some improvements.

There are three steps that every director can take to begin making improvements to the IR function. First, he or she should begin paying attention to IR and learn more about it. How does it work at the company? Who is running it? What are its goals and objectives? How many conference calls does the company hold? Who are the shareholders? The second step is to develop an IR strategy. At a minimum, the board of directors should set strategic capital market goals, since meeting these goals has a considerable impact on shareholder wealth. The third and most important step is to measure the process.

Measuring creates expectations, healthy tensions and pressure, and ultimately, improvement.

We advise using a balanced set of input, process and output measures. An input measure is a measure of what is put into the IR function, and provides an indication of the quality of the firm's commitment to IR. It is possible to measure the number of dollars allocated to the function, the number of people working in the area and the number of hours the CEO spends on IR, for example. These input measures should be complemented by a good set of process measures which indicate how actively the IR function is working, such as the number of conference calls and press releases generated; the number of information requests received; the number of analysts' meetings held; and the number of investor visits sponsored. Finally, it is important to set up output measures — critical, bottom-line measures of what's been achieved. For example, it is relatively easy to measure the numbers of analysts following a company as well as the numbers of institutional and long-term investors. It is also possible to measure share liquidity, volatility and value. A customer-oriented measure can be generated by actively surveying the shareholder constituency. What do the shareholders think? Do they think the company is responsive to requests? Is it comprehensive in its presentations? Do they have suggestions on how to improve the IR function? It may cost a little to collect these data, but the learning can be tremendous.

For too long investor relations has been considered an obligation — a legal, professional and even moral obligation to provide stakeholders with performance and stewardship data. While it is indeed an obligation, the investor relations function should also be treated as an investment with the potential to yield substantial benefits. It's now recognized that changes in disclosure policies can have an impact on trading volumes and prices. Improved communications have also been linked to increases in levels of analyst following and improvements in fundamental share values. For all these reasons, IR should be considered a governance issue. The financial and legal penalties for mismanaged IR are becoming steep, but they're nothing compared to the potential gain from an effective investor relations strategy.

VIII
Leadership: Achieving Exceptional Performance

The Leverage
of Leadership

Jane Howell and Bruce Avolio

*Jane Howell is a professor of
organizational behavior and associate dean of faculty development
at the Richard Ivey School of
Business. Bruce Avolio is a
professor of organizational behavior at Binghamton University.*

How do leaders generate extraordinary performance? Although not all companies or
managers understand the leadership qualities that
produce outstanding performance, the secret to
successful leadership is out. Business researchers have
looked at how three different leadership styles — and
their key behaviors — affect employee and company
performance in organizations around the world.
Studies have involved managers from first-line super-
visors to CEOs, in a variety of settings — from
Fortune 500 companies and startup enterprises to
military, health care and educational organizations.

Comparing Leadership Styles

Studies consistently show that the transformational style of leadership brings tremendous payoffs in business performance and innovation, compared to other leadership styles. These findings are based on a model that identifies the behaviors underlying three leadership styles: transformational, transactional and laissez-faire leadership.

LEADERSHIP AND PERFORMANCE

LEADERSHIP BEHAVIORS		PERFORMANCE
TRANSFORMATIONAL	☞	Beyond Expectations
· Visioning		
· Inspiring		
· Stimulating		
· Coaching		
· Team Building		
TRANSACTIONAL		
· Recognizing	☞	Meets Expectations
· Correcting		Below Expectations
LAISSEZ-FAIRE	☞	Below Expectations
· Avoiding		

Source: Research by Bruce Avolio, Bernard Bass and Jane Howell.

Transformational Leadership

The transformational leader displays a repertoire of behaviors that inspire exceptional performance. The model outlines five key leadership behaviors that have been observed, tested and shown to consistently produce performance results that exceed expectations.

1. *Visioning.* The leader communicates a compelling vision of the future that is widely shared by the organization's members. The vision describes the ultimate outcomes

employees need to achieve. Transformational leaders lead by example and act in ways consistent with the vision.

2. *Inspiring.* The leader communicates the vision with passion, energy and conviction, expresses optimism about the future, and shows enthusiasm about future possibilities. The leader generates excitement in the workplace and heightens others' expectations through symbols and images, which in turn build commitment to the vision.

3. *Stimulating.* The leader arouses interest in new ideas and approaches, and enables employees to think through problems in new ways. The leader who practices intellectual stimulation encourages the rethinking of ideas and the questioning of traditionally accepted ways of doing things. The leader considers "wild" ideas and supports divergent thinking. He or she uses reasoning and analytic thinking to problem-solve and select from the creative ideas generated.

4. *Coaching.* The leader coaches, advises and provides hands-on help for employees to develop their capabilities and improve their performance. He or she listens attentively, understands individual needs, motivations and aspirations, and expresses encouragement, support and confidence in individuals' abilities to meet the expectations inherent in the vision. The leader gives constructive feedback, encourages people to take on greater responsibilities and provides opportunities for development by delegating challenging and interesting tasks.

5. *Team-building.* The leader builds effective teams by selecting team members with complementary skills and encouraging them to work together toward common goals. He or she increases team confidence and commitment by giving positive feedback, sharing information, utilizing individuals' skills and removing obstacles to team performance.

Transactional Leadership

The transactional leader uses both rewards and punishments. This leader provides recognition and rewards when employees meet agreed-upon objectives. Relying on a management-by-objectives approach, he or she communicates performance expectations clearly and celebrates accomplishments when objectives are reached. Although these rewarding/recognizing behaviors result in performance that meets expectations, they rarely result in performance that surpasses them.

Some transactional leaders emphasize correcting more than rewarding. These reactive leaders point out mistakes and criticize performance as their main approach to managing employees. The style of the boss who plays "bad cop," waiting and watching for mistakes to correct, backfires. It results in performance below expectations, and discourages innovation and initiative in the workplace.

This does not mean that leaders should ignore unsatisfactory performance. When performance falls short, an effective leader emphasizes and demonstrates to employees how to meet expectations rather than dwell on mistakes. It is important to monitor the overall ratio of recognizing and rewarding behaviors to correcting behaviors, and strike the right balance between positive and negative feedback. The motivating power of recognition and rewards will be diluted if there is too much focus on employees' shortcomings.

Laissez-Faire Leadership

Some leaders mistakenly believe that the best leadership is the least leadership. Although this leader may think that he or she is empowering employees, this type of leader actually abdicates rather than delegates his or her responsibilities. To employees, these "non-leaders" seem indecisive and indifferent, and are often inaccessible. Not surprisingly, this lack of leadership results in performance well below expectations, low morale, and stifled initiative, creativity and responsibility. This laissez-faire approach is a prescription for failure, where poor leadership equals poor performance.

Multiple Payoffs

Of all the leadership styles, transformational leadership offers the biggest payoff for higher business performance. One of our studies, which surveyed 250 executives and managers at a major financial services company, found that transformational leaders had 34 percent higher business-unit performance results than other types of leader.

Transformational leaders have a strong, positive impact on individual, team and company performance. Further, they develop and encourage employees to achieve higher performance levels.

Studies show that there are many other benefits as well. Transformational leaders are seen as more effective and satisfying to work with and receive higher levels of volunteer effort from employees. They are also more effective under conditions of change. Transformational leaders inspire teams to produce more innovative products and receive more patents for work produced. There are personal payoffs too — transformational leaders receive higher performance appraisal ratings and are promoted more frequently.

How to Be a Transformational Leader

What do all of these studies mean for today's managers? Can people develop the skills to be transformational leaders? The answer is a resounding yes. Our research and experience conducting in-company training programs have proven that outstanding leadership behavior can be developed and sustained over time.

While it may be true that transformational behaviors come more naturally to some people, any manager who is motivated can learn to become a more effective leader by practicing these skills frequently.

Developing Leadership Skills

Although companies demand that their leaders be successful, these leaders may be unaware how their style affects their performance. The first step in developing leadership skills is for managers to gain awareness of how often and how effectively they use the five key behaviors of visioning, inspiring, coaching, stimulating and team-building. Also, they need to consider how often recognizing, correcting and avoiding behaviors are used. Obtaining feedback from direct reports, peers and managers, as well as assessing oneself, are essential for pinpointing leadership strengths and opportunities for development.

After identifying two or three key leadership development priorities, managers need to target particular behaviors for improvement and set specific goals with a time frame in mind. For example, a manager may decide to increase the frequency of coaching behaviors over the next six months by giving direct reports credit for their accomplishments, by offering them assignments to develop their skills, or by conveying confidence in their abilities to reach challenging goals. By practicing these coaching behaviors frequently, managers increase the probability of employees' improved performance.

Organizational Commitment is Key

Personal commitment to becoming a transformational leader is not enough — organizational commitment is also essential. Executives need to recognize that leading by example, serving as a role model and leading by "doing" rather than simply by "telling" are important motivating factors to achieving success. Executives should set challenging development goals and use visioning language, including values, symbols and images, to communicate these goals throughout the organization.

Systems that support transformational behaviors should also be incorporated into the organizational structure. For example, a performance appraisal system that measures and rewards transformational leadership is critical to producing exceptional performance. Further, managers should build innovation into the culture of their business units by encouraging creative ideas, risk-taking and change. Indeed, risk-taking and making mistakes allow learning and innovation to occur.

The Bottom Line

Our research shows that the transformational style of leadership yields substantial bottom-line results. Practicing transformational leadership behaviors is key to developing the next generation of leaders and achieving competitive advantage.

Leadership: Bringing Strategy to Life

Lawrence G. Tapp

Lawrence G. Tapp is Dean of the Richard Ivey School of Business.

There is a significant lack of strategic planning in organizations today. Although talented and intelligent executives spend much time and effort in developing strategic goals, these strategies often fall short as they fail to address the overarching corporate vision.

Strategic plans, no matter how skillfully constructed, are no guarantee of success. Managers at many large organizations put a great deal of energy into their development, but unless the plans are brought to life, very little changes: the bottom line does not improve, and the company does not develop any new competitive advantage. Essentially, the company is no more innovative or profitable than it was at the beginning of the process.

Why is this the case? Perhaps in the midst of gathering and analyzing their data, creators of the corporate plan lost sight of something fundamental and significant: the corporate vision. What is corporate vision? It is not anything that can be distilled onto a piece of paper. In its purest form, vision is the company's reason for being and the employees' reason for caring about what they do.

In most organizations, there are many opportunities to go in several directions at the same time. Resources are dissipated but nothing gets accomplished. A vision provides focus — it serves as a goal to aim for and a way of getting there. There is nothing vague or theoretical about vision; it is the clear, hard reality of things to come.

Vision is most often the product of a handful of exceptional individuals within an organization — individuals who are capable of standing back from the day-to-day melee and seeing beyond the company's functional areas into the future. These people are members of the rare breed known as true leaders. Finding true leaders is one of the most difficult tasks facing any company. As research shows, many of us believe we are effective leaders, but few of us actually measure up in the eyes of our peers and employees.

Leadership is an elusive quality. Researchers, academics and practicing managers have studied and written about it for as long as there has been a discipline of management. Libraries are full of books outlining the essential characteristics of effective leadership. Although there is no shortage of advice on how to become the savior of a company, oddly enough, there are few true leaders.

And yet, leadership is no mystery. Most people agree on a good leader when they see one. And if they think about the people they know who could be described as true leaders, they will likely come up with a list of six or seven outstanding individuals — not all of whom are necessarily CEOs. Leaders can turn up at any level of an organization.

What is so special about good leaders? For one thing, they are thriving in a business world that many find bewildering. In the face of frenzied change in the competitive, regulatory and technological environments, they are calmly pursuing their goals with single-minded purpose. They know where they are going and why — change is simply another curve in the road.

Of course, vision alone does not make a great leader any more than a strategic plan makes a great company. Vision is only as good as its execution. A true leader must be able to take the vision and communicate it to others in the organization in such a way as to inspire them to work toward it. This requires someone with a broad and deep knowledge of their organization and the capacity to understand and motivate others.

It is at this point when strategic planning becomes essential. Once everyone is behind a company's vision, it is time to take the steps toward making it a reality and develop strategic goals. A good strategic plan is like a road map outlining how to get from point A to point B and identifying landmarks and obstacles. Once the plan is in place, leadership breathes life into it, lifts it off the page and places it at the heart of the organization's operation. True leaders have enthusiasm, commitment and boundless energy, and exude a sense of passion and possibility in executing the plan.

Effective leaders also have a knack for finding the right people for the job — and they know how to unleash potential. They are imaginative, flexible, take calculated risks and allow others in the organization to do the same. They are confident enough of their own abilities that they can let employees think and act for themselves. They are skilled in resolving conflict and fostering performance improvement. They create a learning environment where employees can acquire the skills and knowledge they need to bring the company's strategy to life.

Above all, leaders provide a solid ethical base on which to build the organization's vision. They treat all stakeholders —employees, shareholders, board members, suppliers — with respect. And they, in turn, earn respect and trust.

A strategic plan, by itself, is simply a collection of words. However, with the right leadership to bring it to life the corporate strategy can become the road map to success.

Leading from a Distance

Jane Howell and Kate Hall-Merenda

Jane Howell is a professor of organizational behavior and associate dean of faculty development at the Richard Ivey School of Business. Kate Hall-Merenda is a student in Ivey's Ph.D. program.

Leading from a distance is a challenge that a growing number of managers are facing. How can a manager effectively lead employees who work in another city, province or country, or even on another continent? Further, how can he or she motivate them or assess their performance without ongoing face-to-face contact?

Globalization and Technology

As globalization accelerates and multinationals proliferate, more managers are being expected to lead employees located in different countries and time zones. And managing people across the ocean presents a considerably different set of challenges than managing them from down the hall.

Advances in telecommunication and computing technologies are permitting a growing number of employees to work away from the office. Virtual offices, and even virtual organizations, are increasingly adding to the physical distance separating leaders and followers.

Managers are also being asked to lead other firms' employees. As organizations downsize and contract out work that used to be done in-house, or engage in strategic alliances, leaders are spending more of their time managing employees across organizations.

Out of Sight, Out of Mind

Physical distance creates many potential problems which leaders ignore at their peril. Out of sight can easily be interpreted as out of mind. Employees may feel isolated or forgotten, and wonder if their leader cares. They may respond by slacking off or simply going through the motions of work, and poor performance often results.

How does a leader develop, motivate and evaluate a follower who works in a different country or city? How can he or she close the distance gap? Our research set out to understand the impact of both physical distance and the leader-follower relationship on follower performance and which, if any, leadership behaviors contribute to outstanding performance despite the distance factor.

Closer Is Better

A survey of 109 business leaders and 371 followers in a large financial institution suggests that physical distance does make it more difficult for managers and employees to build and sustain high-quality working relationships. In close leadership situations, managers have a greater opportunity to support their employees and to show individualized concern for them. Proximity permits the development of trust through frequent personal interaction.

The question is, can leaders close the distance gap and establish productive relationships with followers?

Bridging the Gap

Although physical distance can make leading more difficult, it is possible to develop exceptional leader-follower relationships. Further, employees who have excellent relationships with their leaders can deliver outstanding performance despite being in different locations.

This is a powerful finding with an important message for leaders and their employees: when managers and employees share common goals and are part of a healthy relationship, employees are able to transcend geographic distance and pursue the business unit's mission and goals. In essence, shared values help to buffer physical distance.

How do leaders foster and sustain this type of relationship? Employees who rated their relationship with their manager as high-quality also noted that their managers frequently engaged in "transformational" leadership behaviors, which include visioning, inspiring, stimulating, coaching and team-building. And these leaders, in turn, inspire outstanding follower performance.

Yet, distance continues to be a challenge, even for transformational leaders. Employees who are in the same location as their managers are more likely to deliver outstanding performance than those who are not. Some transformational behaviors, such as coaching, are more difficult to achieve when team members are not located in the same place. Indeed, proximity enhances opportunities to coach or intellectually stimulate employees.

Far-Reaching Benefits

However, there are some transformational behaviors that leaders can use to bridge the distance and performance gaps. Articulating a compelling vision of the future can stimulate employees in different locations to achieve outstanding performance. Communicating that vision in an inspiring way and asking questions that prompt employees to think about striving toward the vision in different ways are particularly important when managing from a distance. And each of these behaviors can be set in motion without the manager and employee necessarily being in the same location — they can be just as effectively carried out through alternative communication media.

Recent trends predict that physical distance between leaders and their employees will be a major issue in the next millennium. Leaders will need to be proactive in finding solutions to this potentially costly problem. Since effective relationships supported by transformational leadership behaviors provide one solution to this problem, we recommend that managers make relationship-building a top priority. The benefits of quality relationships far outweigh the efforts involved in developing them.

The Ties That Bind

To lead effectively from a distance, leaders must make the ongoing effort to establish and maintain healthy and productive relationships with their employees. Visioning, inspiring, coaching and stimulating are powerful tools managers can use to build and sustain high-quality relationships and transcend distance barriers. Long-distance leaders who are encouraging and who communicate a shared vision to their employees are setting the stage for outstanding results.

Being a Supportive Leader

Chris Higgins and Linda Duxbury

Chris Higgins is a professor of management science and information systems at the Richard Ivey School of Business. Linda Duxbury is a business professor at Carleton University.

Economic realities are restructuring the needs of today's workforce. How managers respond to these changes can have a substantial impact on employee commitment and overall company performance.

Thirty years ago, most Canadian households relied on one wage earner. Today, economic changes are forcing most Canadian families to have both partners in the workforce. Recent statistics from the Vanier Institute show that almost 70 percent of mothers whose youngest child is between three and five years old are in the labor force, as are more than 75 percent of the mothers of school-aged children. Additionally, Canada's population is ageing, and more individuals are responsible for the care of their elderly parents. The bottom line for these economic and social realities is that organizations are employing a workforce that has significant problems balancing work, family and personal demands.

The situation in the United States is quite similar. According to the Families and Work Institute's 1997 National Study of the Changing Workforce, the proportion of employees living in dual-earner families has increased markedly in the past 20 years. According to this study, in more than 75 percent of couples, both partners work full time. Thus, among married employees, the pooled time available for childcare and household work is decreasing, creating additional stresses off the job. The study also reported that employed men and women have less time for themselves than they did 20 years ago, lower personal well-being and greater negative spillover from their job into their home life.

Three conclusions resulted from our research study involving more than 50,000 Canadians. First, while the demographics of the Canadian workforce have changed dramatically in the past two decades, many employers have not changed how they structure work and manage their workforce. Second, a large percentage of Canadian employees have excessive levels of work-family conflict. For example, our research shows that 56 percent of employees with high levels of work-family conflict suffer high levels of job stress. Comparatively, only 19 percent of employees with low work-family conflict suffer high levels of stress. More important, and directly affecting the bottom line, are the data on absenteeism. Individuals with high work-family conflict average eight days of absenteeism per year, compared to three for those experiencing low levels of conflict.

Third, there is a tremendous amount of inequity in organizations as managers act as gatekeepers to many of the benefits offered by firms. Who an employee works for within an organization often becomes more important than where they work. For example, many organizations offer flexible work arrangements and family-friendly benefits. It appears, however, that not all employees are using and benefiting from these policies equally.

Identifying key supportive and non-supportive behaviors can provide organizations with a useful tool to use in the performance appraisal process, promotion decisions, managerial education programs, upward feedback exercises and sensitivity training. We developed a methodology where organizations identify those behaviors associated with supportive or non-supportive management. The methodology has several strengths. First, it focuses on behaviors, not attitudes — as behaviors are specific and can be observed and counted. Second, the perceptions of what makes a supportive manager vary across individuals and organizations. Since our method is customized, it allows each organization to identify their unique core behaviors.

What Is a Supportive Manager?

Although no two managers are alike, there are common traits that characterize supportive managers. Supportive managers engage in two-way communication with their subordinates, provide positive feedback, mentor their employees, allow employees autonomy, recognize that employees have a life outside work and facilitate the completion of job tasks. Non-supportive managers are poor interpersonal communicators, do not show respect for employees, focus on hours of work rather than output and behave inconsistently.

Although most of these supportive and non-supportive characteristics appear throughout many organizations, the relative importance of each characteristic depends on the organizational culture, the gender of the employee and the type of job performed. For example, women are significantly more likely than men to appreciate a manager who mentors them and engages in two-way communication; managers are more likely than non-managers to perceive a supervisor who offers them support in private and then disowns them in a public forum as non-supportive; and public sector employees are more likely to focus on behaviors dealing with respect than are their private sector counterparts.

A common reaction to these results is that they are hardly revolutionary. All managers should be supportive. And besides, why should an organization worry about how supportive their managers are as long as the work gets done?

There are a number of important reasons why organizations should pay attention to management behavior. First, the majority of managers are not highly supportive — only one-third to one-half of the employees we surveyed gave their managers high marks on the supportive scale. Second, our data suggest that supportive behaviors are linked to valued organizational outcomes. Employees with supportive managers are more likely to have high job satisfaction, high organizational commitment and lower levels of job stress, absenteeism and life stress. They are also more likely to feel that the organizational policies of their company are supportive of them. This finding is particularly interesting as the organizational policies were the same for both groups in the study — the only difference was in how the policies were implemented. Finally, employees who work for managers who display supportive rather than non-supportive behaviors are also more likely to feel secure about their jobs, trust their managers and engage in upward feedback. Such impressions are critical success factors for leaders who wish to successfully implement change, such as re-engineering how work is done or restructuring their organizations.

Supportive managers have a positive effect on both the organization and the employee. The companies involved in this research have various initiatives underway to change their managerial climate in this direction, including aligning the organization's reward system toward supportive behaviors, recognizing managers who are supportive, basing hiring and promotion decisions on supportive managerial behaviors and conducting regular "pulse taking" surveys and 360-degree feedback sessions.

Change is here to stay. The question is: how are managers responding? A responsive and flexible approach to managing a workforce not only creates a healthier work environment, it yields returns that far outweigh the costs of managing change.

The methodology used to define supportive and non-supportive management behaviors has been employed in more than 10 organizations. Paul Smith, senior vice-president, human resources at BC Telecom talks about the company's experience with supportive management research:

"BC Telecom first started to focus its energy on supportive management in 1994. The driving force behind this activity was the need for our organization to change very quickly from a monopoly culture to one that sustained and supported aggressive competition. BC Telecom's supportive management objectives were incorporated into the balanced scorecard in order to hold the senior management team accountable for creating a supportive work environment. A percentage of each executive's variable compensation is awarded only when specific targets are met. The initial research into supportive management proved that there is a direct correlation between the environment created by a supportive manager and the impact on the quality of service that is delivered to customers.

"In 1994, we had 36 percent supportive managers; by 1997, we were up to 59 percent. Our long-term objective to the year 2000 is to have zero non-supportive managers in our organization.

"One of BC Telecom's primary objectives in moving from a monopoly to an open-market organization was to ensure that it create an environment that empowers employees to make customer-focused decisions without having to seek permission through the organizational hierarchy. BC Telecom acknowledges that, in a highly competitive environment, it is imperative that employees are empowered to make independent and immediate decisions that enhance customer value. The correlation between an environment that allows fast-paced decision-making and supportive management has been proven over the four-year period since the company first began this work."

John Lahey, senior vice-president, Ontario southwest region, CIBC, shares his experiences with supportive management:

"In 1995, CIBC conducted a study on leadership behaviors with Duxbury and Higgins. The results were fascinating. They showed that leaders' personal behaviors had a significant impact on organizational outcomes such as productivity, morale, stress and organizational commitment. The impact was far more than we suspected.

"Shortly after completing the study, I was transferred to a line-banking role where I had the opportunity to use the findings in real life. My conclusion after two years — it really works. It works because it's simple, it's observable and it's behavioral.

"In my new job, I have to be a role model of supportive management. It's tough because you realize very quickly how difficult it is to be consistently supportive. It's very easy to take the path of least resistance. Recently, I have focused on recruitment — taking every opportunity to hire naturally supportive managers. Today, our business results have improved significantly and continue to show steady progress. I attribute a lot of this success to the emphasis on supportive management. It helps create an atmosphere of trust, confidence and commitment, essential to high-performing teams."

Managing Change:
Checking the Red
Queen

David K. Hurst

David K. Hurst is a speaker, consultant and writer on management and a research fellow at the Richard Ivey School of Business. He is also the author of Crisis & Renewal: Meeting the Challenge of Organizational Change *(Harvard Business School Press, 1995).*

Time is an organization's most precious resource. Unlike all other resources, however, its flow is hard to measure and its stock cannot be stored. Too often it is either used carelessly or squandered completely. Firms routinely commit themselves to major projects and multiple action plans that identify every resource except the scarcest — people's time.

Once it seemed that people had enough slack in their schedules to handle a firm's failure to take time into consideration. But this is no longer the case. The upturn in the business cycle may have diverted management attention from downsizing to growth, but the pace of work is, if anything, more frenetic than ever. And technology has made things worse. Many observers have suggested that the principal effect of the increased use of information technology in the workplace has transported workers to the "realm of the Red Queen," the character in Lewis Carroll's *Through the Looking Glass* who says to Alice, "here ... it takes all the running you can do to keep in the same place." With the shortages created by downsizing and the responsibilities imposed by empowerment, workers' attention has never been more fragmented. Indeed, the need to prioritize and integrate the complex workings of organizations has never been greater. Yet most management tools are inadequate for the task. Priorities cannot be spelled out in advance from the top as issues are much too complex and dynamic, and people are too scattered.

One cause of this problem is the discontinuity that managers create between the corporation's present and its past, as illustrated during the recent recession when countless companies tried a variety of management change techniques ranging from reengineering to empowerment. The use of these kinds of methods stretches back as far as one can remember, yet the managers who implement them seemed to have no memory at all of their previous attempts. For the most part, each initiative is introduced from scratch — as if the previous programs never existed. There is rarely any discussion of what did or did not work in the past, and no review of the fate of the projects and the people involved. It is as if the organization is a blank slate upon which new messages are to be written.

Discontinuity between past and present is also characteristic of acquisitions. When one Canadian insurance company acquired another, their first step was to bring in an American consulting firm notorious for its tough reengineering programs. Nothing could have done more damage to the cultural core of the acquired company and its people. Of all management techniques, business reengineering more than any other holds no regard for the past with its "starting over with a clean sheet" designs. Although some managers find them attractive, these claims are troubling for many employees: the corporation may not remember, but the employees do. All too often, like Winston Smith, the central figure in George Orwell's *1984*, employees experience a deep sense of disorientation. They can clearly remember important initiatives to which managers once demanded their complete attention and wholehearted commitment. Now they feel that their memories of these earlier events are dysfunctional. Any questions about the fate of the people and their projects are not only unwelcome, but misinterpreted as "resisting change," attracting sanctions from the all powerful "Inner Party" — the ruling elite.

At best, people become confused and unsettled, able to understand individual events, but unable to connect them — unable to understand what is happening. At worst, like Winston Smith, they develop a profound cynicism. On the surface, while the "thought police" are around, they become masters at giving the appearance of the "buy in." However, this is only lip service as they wait for the program's inevitable failure and its replacement by yet another set of change techniques.

What can managers do to counter this vicious cycle? How can they keep the Red Queen at bay? There are some specific techniques that can be used to measure and economize people's time. Intel, for example, is firm about the effectiveness of its internal meetings, and has clear specifications for them. But mere technique can neither focus an organization nor generate commitment. Genuine commitment to change requires that people make sense of who they are and where they have been. But today it is difficult to do. Our society is so deluged by data, so inundated with information, that meaning becomes fragmented. For employees to focus on new activities over a lengthy period of time, there has to be some coherence to their tasks. It is not enough for managers to hold out a vision of the future; their employees have to make sense of the present and that requires that it be connected with the past. Meaning in their daily lives is found in the integration of what they are doing now, where they have been and where they are going.

Throughout history the primary vehicle for connecting with others and piecing together disparate events has been the story. Stories tell of change through time and teach those who listen to them about the experiences of others. They allow the ability to reconnect events, to reconstruct meaning and to understand what has happened. Stories, like music, are about memory and feeling, continually reminding the audience of the role played by the past in the present: they teach people about time. To tell a story is an act of leadership, for, again like music, a story is more important for the context it creates than the content it delivers. Through the use of stories, leaders can create between vision and history a present where there is a sense of evolution and progress. Here there is a space in time that can become full of meaning for the people in the organization — a sense of permanence in a pattern of change. Indeed, every time leaders tell their organization's story they help others make sense of who they are. It is precisely this sense of permanence that is the organization's identity. And with its articulation, events and activities take on a new significance for people. The organization's identity acts as the touchstone for determining its priorities, and is a catalyst for self-organization allowing workers to manage priorities and benefit the entire system.

If this is the case, why do so many organizations deny their past and why are their managers so reluctant to look back at their previous attempts at change? In *1984* the "Party" manipulated the past to maintain control. They achieved this by keeping the "proles," the masses, in a constant state of threat from newly created enemies. "Who controls the past controls the future; who controls the present controls the past," ran the Party slogan.

Perhaps the dynamics are similar in modern organizations. Clearly a heightened sense of urgency is critical at the beginning of any change program, and what better than a controlled crisis to mobilize the troops? If past attempts at change have failed, why consider them? That may detract from a new approach. But this would be true only if the past could be wiped clean from memory, just as it was in Orwell's vision. Unfortunately, for such managers it cannot. Indeed it would not be desirable, even if it were possible, for people learn far more from error than from success. To deny the past is to refuse to learn from it, and this is dangerous. The failure of previous change initiatives often points to subtle systemic barriers that constrain an organization's ability to change. The organization has to be released from these constraints if any change is to take effect. Some firms, for example, create myriad task forces without clear mandates and boundaries. As a result, senior management demands frequent formal updates. The task forces spend the bulk of their time either preparing presentations or waiting to see the boss.

Managers who develop coherent organizational stories to frame their change initiatives will also find them enormously helpful in that they force managers to be much more selective in the programs they adopt. Organizations such as Dofasco, Hewlett-Packard and 3M, who have a strong sense of their history, are circumspect in their choice of change programs. Their stories act as filters, allowing them either to discard certain change techniques or limit their use. If a particular technique does not fit with the story, then it is either inappropriate to the organization or the timing is wrong. Further, it will scarcely make sense to those who are to implement it.

Managers of organizations without stories to tell run the risk of becoming totally incoherent in their change efforts — confused in perception and muddled in practice. Without a sense of who they are and where they have been, they are unable to understand the relevance of each technique to their particular situations. Instead they try to introduce one approach after another to their confused organizations. Incapable of distinguishing inputs from outputs, they end up slaves to fad and fashion, trying to replicate the practices of "excellent" companies in contexts they cannot support. It is the "freedom" from the important that makes people slaves to the urgent — pawns of the Red Queen. Santayana could have been thinking of modern organizations when he wrote, "Progress, far from consisting of change, depends on retentiveness. . . .Those who cannot remember the past are condemned to repeat it."

Creating a Winning Team

Alexander Mikalachki

Alexander Mikalachki is a professor of organizational behavior at the Richard Ivey School of Business.

O ur society is inundated with teams: sports teams that compete for titles and fill the sports pages, self-managed work teams that cut through the ineffectiveness of silo-like divisional or functional group structures, and even families, which are viewed as teams in which members depend on one another for survival and growth. In effect, much of our life takes place as a team member. But what makes a winning team? Drawing on similarities between characteristics of sports and work teams offers some insights into the ingredients for what it takes to be a winner.

Sports teams, given their visibility and scrutiny, allow us insight into differentiating winning teams from losing ones. After a championship has been decided, winners and losers tend to respond predictably. Team members on the victorious side, when interviewed, tend to use the "we" pronoun ("We worked together as a team"), they feel peak levels of elation, they perform their roles well and their coaches have a good game plan. Losers tend to use the "I" pronoun ("I am proud of my players"), experience profound disappointment, congratulate the winner and might refer to their hopes of winning in the future ("Wait until next year").

In their book *The Wisdom of Teams*, Jon Katzenbach and Douglas Smith differentiate winning task teams from losing ones. They note that winning teams tend to be small in number (20 members or fewer), and have members whose skills are complementary. They share a purpose and are mutually accountable for attaining their goals. There is also a common understanding of the team's approach to their task: roles are understood, relationships are clear and the rewards of success are shared equally.

Successful sports teams and management task teams have in common team cohesion, a game plan strategy and an identification with clear, achievable goals. To be a winning team, it is necessary to establish the conditions that achieve cohesion and to gain members' commitment to strategic and organizational goals as opposed to social or personal ones.

Making a Team Cohesive

Cohesion involves three conditions. First, there must be an opportunity for interaction. Team size, the freedom of movement and flexibility in altering one's role affect the opportunity to interact. The second condition is the team members' role interdependence. The higher the dependence of one member's role on the actions of other members, the greater the likelihood of cohesion. The third condition is the positive regard that team members have for each other. The greater the acceptance of individual differences and the concern for each member's well-being, the greater the likelihood of cohesion.

A few years ago, an NFL football defensive football coach threw a punch at his own team's offensive coach after a particular play. Although a glancing punch causing no physical harm, commentators lamented the act for the rest of the game. It was not the punch itself that concerned people, as much as it symbolized internal strife and negative regard among team members. Interestingly, the team lost its next game after an 11-game winning streak.

Developing a Game Plan

To be a winner in either a work or a sports environment, a cohesive team must have a viable game plan or strategy. The plan considers the nature of the task, the skills available among team members, the strength of the competitive or resisting forces and the goals to be achieved.

An effective plan encourages interaction. It uses the resources of team members, and synergistic benefits are produced as their unique skills are interlocked. The commitment to the plan by each member allows maximum flexibility, innovation and a low need for external direction and mediating activities. As team members have input to the plan, and the ability to modify and direct it, their commitment heightens.

Clear Goals Improve Performance

Goal-setting is another important factor in making a team a winner. One of the most important behavioral science research findings is that the setting of achievable goals by individuals or by formal leaders significantly increases the level of production. Measurable goals, whether the result of a consensus process involving team members and leaders or imposed by leaders, generate higher levels of performance.

Teams and individuals can set different goals — for example, winning a title, restructuring an organization, or getting promoted. It is important to differentiate task goals (restructuring an organization, winning a championship) from social or personal goals (getting promoted). Task goals essentially aim to benefit the organization and each team member. In all teams, some members contribute talents that are highly valued and result in greater compensation. Quarterbacks are paid more than linemen, engineers more than draftsmen. However, bonuses earned by teams must be shared equally. To do otherwise would seriously undermine performance.

A Canadian construction company gave bonuses to its trades teams based on their profit performance. One of the teams, however, thought the share of profit attributed to it was too low and that consequently its performance bonus was lower than that paid to other teams. Discontent over this led to the company losing a contract. The whole company lost because one team's personal goals were in conflict with the organization's goals.

The key to setting in motion the important components of cohesion, strategy and goal commitment is effective leadership. By selecting the right people, designing an appropriate plan and establishing achievable goals, leaders generate the ingredients necessary to create a winning team.

ORGANIZATION INDEX

PERSON INDEX

SUBJECT INDEX

NOTES

NOTES

NOTES

NOTES